WRITE YOUR WAY

A COMPREHENSIVE GUIDE TO PERSONAL GROWTH AND SELF-EXPRESSION THROUGH JOURNALING

THE JOURNALING MASTERY SERIES: THEORY AND PRACTICE

BOOK 2

RICHARD FRENCH

Indie Pen Press
Seattle, Washington USA
IndiePenPress.com

Second Edition: December 2024

Paperback ISBN: 979-8-9919463-1-5

CONTENTS

ONE
THE POWER OF THE PEN (OR KEYBOARD)

Sarah's hand hovered over the blank page; her new leather-bound journal open before her. The faint scent of fresh paper mingled with the aroma of her chamomile tea. Outside, the city was slowly waking up, the soft light of dawn creeping through her apartment window.

She took a deep breath and began to write:

"I feel silly doing this. It's like I'm back in middle school, starting with 'Dear Diary.' But my psychologist says it might help with the anxiety, so here goes nothing..."

As Sarah's pen moved across the page, she joined a tradition as old as writing itself. In a musty library across town, a graduate student named Mike turned the pages of Marcus Aurelius *'Meditations'* with care, the ancient Roman emperor's personal reflections never meant for publication.

In a high school classroom, a teenager named Zoe scribbled her pen racing across a notebook emblazoned with stickers, channeling the spirit of Anne Frank, whose diary became a powerful testament to resilience in the face of unimaginable adversity.

Across the ocean, in a sun-drenched studio, an artist named Carlos sketched and wrote in a battered sketchbook, inspired by the vibrant journals of Frida Kahlo, where art and words intertwined to express her innermost thoughts and experiences.

But what exactly were Sarah, Mike, Zoe, and Carlos doing? Was it simply keeping a diary, or was there more to it?

Let's peek over a few more shoulders to find out:

In a sleek downtown office, Tom, a busy executive, started his day by opening his laptop. His fingers flew across the keyboard as he typed out three pages of stream-of-consciousness thoughts. He called it his "brain dump," a digital decluttering of his mind before diving into the day's challenges.

"I'm worried about the Johnson account... Need to remember to pick up dry cleaning... Why did I agree to that dinner party on Saturday? ... Focus, Tom, focus..."

As he finished, Tom felt a sense of clarity wash over him. The anxieties that had been swirling in his mind now sat neatly on the screen, somehow less daunting when seen in black and white.

In a cozy apartment filled with plants, Amira sat cross-legged on her bed, surrounded by a chaos of colored pens, washi tape, and magazine clippings. Her journal lay open before her, its pages a riot of color and texture.

Amira pasted a photo of a serene beach scene onto the page. Next to it, she wrote in swirling blue ink:

"I long for the peace of this place. The sound of waves, the feel of sand between my toes. One day, I'll get there. For now, I'll carry this calm within me."

For Amira, journaling was a playground for creativity, a space where words and images danced together to express what she couldn't quite say out loud.

In a bustling coffee shop, Carlos, a high school student, hunched over a bullet journal, its pages filled with neat lists and tracker boxes drawn with precision. He added a checkmark to his "Daily Meditation" box, then flipped to his goals page.

"Run 5K without stopping," he read. With a smile, he drew a bold line through the goal and wrote next to it: "Completed 5/15/24!" A sense of accomplishment surged through him as he set his next running goal.

As diverse as these practices were, they all fell under the umbrella of journaling. At its core, journaling is a conversation with oneself, captured on paper or screen.

But does it actually work? Is there science behind the anecdotes?

In a university laboratory, Dr. James Pennebaker, a psychologist at the University of Texas, pored over the results of his latest study. Participants who had written about traumatic experiences for just 15 minutes a day over four days showed better immune function and fewer doctor visits in the following months.

"Fascinating," he murmured, jotting down notes for his next paper. His groundbreaking research showed that expressive writing could lead to improved mental and physical health.

Across the campus, a group of researchers huddled around a computer screen, analyzing the results of their 2018 study published in the Journal of Medical Internet Research. They found that online positive affect journaling (focusing on positive experiences) led to decreased mental distress and increased well-being after just one month.

"Look at these fMRI scans," one researcher exclaimed, pointing to a series of brain images. Their 2020 study had shown that expressive writing activated regions in the brain associated with emotional regulation and self-reflection. "It's not just psychological," she said, "we're literally seeing the brain change."

As the sun climbed higher in the sky, Sarah set down her pen and closed her journal. She stretched, surprised to find that an hour had passed. The anxious knot in her stomach had loosened somewhat. She couldn't explain it, but something had shifted. With a small smile, she tucked the journal into her bag. Tomorrow, she would write again.

Across the city, and indeed across the world, countless others were doing the same. Each in their own way, they were discovering the power of putting pen to paper (or fingers to keyboard). They were unlocking the potential of their own minds, one page at a time.

What story will you write?

TWO
YOUR JOURNALING TOOLKIT

Maya's fingers trailed along the shelves of "Inkwell Dreams," the local stationery store. The scent of leather and paper enveloped her as she wandered the aisles, eyes wide with possibility. Leather-bound notebooks, sleek gel pens, and washi tape in every color imaginable vied for her attention. How was she supposed to choose?

"Can I help you find anything?" a friendly voice asked. Maya turned to see Eliza, the store owner, her grey hair tied back in a messy bun, ink stains on her fingers.

"I'm starting a journal," Maya explained, "but I'm not sure what I need."

Eliza's eyes lit up. "Ah, a new journaler! Well, let's start with the basics. Are you thinking paper or digital?"

It's a question every modern journaler faces: traditional or tech? Let's explore both options through Maya's journey.

THE TACTILE EXPERIENCE: PAPER JOURNALING

Maya picked up a soft leather journal, its pages thick and creamy. As she ran her hand over the cover, she remembered the satisfying scratch of pen against paper from her school days.

"There's something special about writing by hand, isn't there?" Eliza mused. "Did you know that students who take notes by hand retain information better than those who type?"

Maya raised an eyebrow, intrigued.

Eliza continued, "Dr. Virginia Clinton, a professor of education, found that handwriting engages different cognitive processes. It's not just about recording information; it's about processing it."

Maya opened the journal, imagining her thoughts flowing onto its pages. But a doubt nagged at her. "What if I make a mistake? Or want to reorganize my thoughts?"

Eliza chuckled. "That's the beauty of journaling, dear. It's not about perfection. It's about the process."

Still, Maya couldn't help but think of her cluttered apartment. Where would she store years of journals?

THE DIGITAL ADVANTAGE

As if reading her mind, Eliza gestured to a sleek tablet on display. "Of course, digital journaling has its perks too."

Maya picked up the tablet, surprised by its lightness. With a few taps, she opened a journaling app. The interface was clean and intuitive, with features like password protection, cloud syncing, and multimedia integration.

"I can see the appeal," Maya admitted. "Being able to search through old entries would be handy."

Eliza nodded. "Many of my customers swear by their digital journals. John, a consultant who comes in for pen refills, told me he jots down thoughts on his phone while waiting for the train, then fleshes them out on his laptop later."

Maya could imagine the convenience. No more lugging around a heavy notebook or scrambling for a pen when inspiration struck.

"But," Eliza added with a knowing smile, "some find digital interfaces distracting. And there's always the question of privacy. How comfortable are you with your deepest thoughts living in the cloud?"

Maya bit her lip, considering. Both options had their merits. How to choose?

THE HYBRID APPROACH

"You know," Eliza said, noting Maya's indecision, "many journalers end up adopting a hybrid approach."

She led Maya to a display showcasing both traditional and tech journaling tools. "You might use a paper journal for deep, reflective writing sessions at home while keeping a notes app handy for quick thoughts on the go."

Maya's eyes lit up. "I could have the best of both worlds!"

Eliza beamed. "Exactly! Journaling is a personal journey. The best tools are the ones you'll actually use."

CREATING YOUR JOURNALING SPACE

As Maya left the store, her arms full of supplies she had selected with care, her mind was already racing with possibilities. At home, she cleared a corner of her desk, adding a small potted succulent and a scented candle.

She arranged her new journal and pens just so, then opened her laptop to set up her digital journaling app. Already, this little corner felt like a sanctuary, a space just for her thoughts.

Maya settled into her chair, took a deep breath, and began to write. The words flowed easier than she expected, a mix of typing and handwriting that felt natural and free.

In that moment, Maya realized that the tools were just that – tools. The real magic of journaling lay in the act itself, in showing up day after day to connect with herself.

As the candle flickered and the city hummed outside her window, Maya smiled. This was just the beginning of her journaling journey, and she couldn't wait to see where it would lead.

Remember, your journaling practice is unique to you. Whether you prefer the smell of ink or the glow of a screen, the coziness of a reading nook, or the energy of a busy café, the most important thing is to create a space – both physical and mental – where you can show up and connect with yourself.

As you embark on your own journaling adventure, consider these factors:

1. **Comfort**: Choose a supportive chair and good lighting for longer writing sessions.
2. **Privacy**: Select a spot where you feel safe expressing yourself freely.
3. **Inspiration**: Surround yourself with objects or images that spark creativity.
4. **Accessibility**: Keep your journaling tools easily available to reduce barriers to writing.

And remember, it's okay to experiment and change your setup as you go. Your journaling practice will likely evolve over time, and your toolkit can evolve with it.

Now, armed with the knowledge of different journaling tools and approaches, what will your journaling space look like? How will you blend the traditional and the digital in your practice? The page – be it paper or pixel – awaits your unique voice.

THREE
FINDING YOUR FLOW – JOURNALING TECHNIQUES FOR BEGINNERS

Emma stared at the blank page, pen hovering uncertainly. The gentle ticking of her bedside clock seemed to mock her hesitation. "I want to start journaling," she had told her therapist last week, "but I never know what to write." Now, faced with the reality of the empty page, those words echoed in her mind.

Sound familiar? Don't worry – writer's block happens to everyone, especially when you're just starting out. Let's explore some techniques to get those words flowing, following Emma's journey as she discovers her journaling voice.

1. STREAM OF CONSCIOUSNESS WRITING

Emma set her phone timer for 5 minutes, took a deep breath, and began to write whatever came to mind:

"This is stupid I don't know what to write about maybe I should give up no keep going what's that noise outside probably just the neighbor's cat I wonder if I remembered to buy cat food I need to make a grocery list focus

Emma you're supposed to be journaling what does that even mean I guess I'm doing it now these are my thoughts on paper weird..."

As the timer chimed, Emma blinked in surprise. Her page was full of rambling thoughts, but she felt a sense of release. It wasn't Shakespeare, but it was a start.

Tip: Don't worry about grammar, spelling, or even making sense. The goal is to bypass your inner critic and tap into your subconscious.

2. GRATITUDE JOURNALING

The next evening, Emma decided to try a different approach. She'd read about the benefits of gratitude, so she titled her page "Three Things I'm Grateful For" and began to write:

1. *"The way the sunlight hit the trees on my walk this morning, making everything look golden.*
2. *My sister calling just to check in.*
3. *Finding that last piece of chocolate I forgot about in the back of the cupboard."*

As she wrote, Emma felt a subtle shift in her mood. The stress of her day seemed to recede as she focused on these positive moments.

Research Note: Dr. Robert Emmons, a leading gratitude researcher, has found that practicing gratitude can increase happiness and life satisfaction. In a 2003 study published in the Journal of Personality and Social Psychology, Emmons and McCullough found that participants who kept gratitude journals reported higher levels of positive emotions and better sleep quality.

3. PROMPT-BASED WRITING

On a day when Emma felt stuck, she turned to a list of journaling prompts she'd found online. One caught her eye: "What's the best thing that happened today?" She began to write:

"The best thing that happened today was nailing that presentation at work. I was so nervous, but all the preparation paid off. I felt confident and articulate, and my boss even complimented me afterward. It's a small win, but it feels good to be recognized for my hard work."

As she wrote, Emma found herself delving deeper into her feelings about work, her aspirations, and her self-confidence. The prompt had sparked a rich vein of self-reflection she hadn't expected.

Tip: Keep a list of prompts handy for days when you need a little nudge. Websites like "Journal Buddies" offer hundreds of free prompts for all ages and situations.

4. REFLECTION ON MEDIA

After finishing a novel that had deeply moved her, Emma felt compelled to write about it:

"I just finished 'The Midnight Library' by Matt Haig. The idea of being able to see all the different paths your life could have taken is fascinating. It made me think about my own choices and regrets. But ultimately, the book's message about appreciating the life you have really struck a chord. I want to focus more on being present and grateful for my current reality, rather than always wondering 'what if?'"

This entry led Emma to reflect on her own life choices and values, sparking a deeper level of introspection than she'd experienced before.

Tip: Writing about books, movies, podcasts, or art that resonates with you can be a great way to explore your own thoughts and feelings.

5. BULLET JOURNALING

Intrigued by the bullet journaling system she'd seen on social media, Emma decided to give it a try. She created a simple spread:

March 15, 2024

- *Call the dentist to schedule cleaning*
- *Buy birthday gift for Mom*
- *Finish report for work project*
> *Start daily meditation practice*
* *Had a great catch-up coffee with Alex*
* *Feeling anxious about an upcoming presentation*

Emma found the structured approach freeing. She could jot down tasks, events, and feelings all in one place, giving her a bird's-eye view of her day.

Research Note: A 2020 study published in the Journal of Environmental Psychology found that writing tasks down can free up cognitive resources, reducing anxiety and improving performance. The researchers dubbed this the "intention offloading" effect.

6. DIALOGUING

On a day when Emma felt conflicted about a decision she had to make, she tried a technique her therapist had suggested: dialoguing with herself. She wrote out a conversation between her "logical" side and her "emotional" side:

Logical Emma: We should take that new job offer. It's a great opportunity for career growth.

Emotional Emma: But I'm scared. What if I'm not good enough? What if I fail?

Logical Emma: We've succeeded in challenging situations before. Remember the Johnson project?

Emotional Emma: That's true. I did handle that well...

As the dialogue unfolded, Emma gained clarity on her fears and motivations, helping her approach the decision with more self-awareness.

7. MIND MAPPING

When Emma's thoughts felt tangled, she turned to mind mapping. In the center of a blank page, she wrote "My Ideal Future" and began branching out with related ideas:

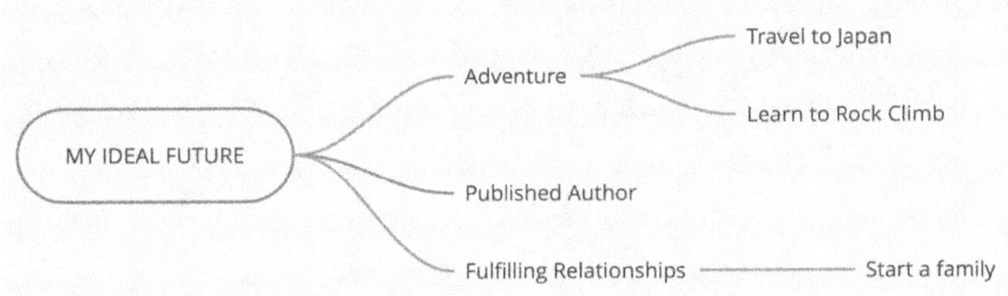

The visual representation helped Emma see connections between her various goals and dreams, sparking new insights about what she valued.

Tech Tip: For digital journalers, apps like MindMeister or XMind offer robust mind-mapping tools that can be integrated with journaling practices.

As weeks passed, Emma found herself reaching for her journal more frequently. Some days she wrote pages; other days, just a few lines. She experimented with different techniques, finding some that resonated deeply and others that didn't quite fit her style.

She began to view her journal not as a chore or an assignment, but as a conversation with herself - a space for exploration, reflection, and growth.

Remember, there's no "right" way to journal. The techniques presented here are just starting points. As you begin your own journaling journey, feel free to experiment, combine approaches, or invent entirely new ways of engaging with your thoughts and feelings on the page.

The most important thing is to show up and write. Your unique voice and style will emerge over time. So, grab your pen (or open your app), take a deep breath, and let your thoughts flow. Your journal is waiting to meet you.

FOUR
DEVELOPING YOUR JOURNALING PRACTICE

The alarm blared, jolting Alex awake. 5:30 AM. He groaned, tempted to hit snooze, but then remembered his commitment. With a sigh, he dragged himself out of bed, shuffled to his desk, and opened his journal.

Day 1 of journaling. Here goes nothing...

Developing a journaling practice is like growing a garden. It takes time, patience, and consistent care. But with dedication, it can blossom into something beautiful and nourishing. Let's follow Alex's journey as he cultivates his journaling habit.

FINDING YOUR RHYTHM

Week 1:

Alex stared at the blank page, pen hovering uncertainly. What should he write about? After a few moments of hesitation, he began:

I'm not sure what I'm doing. This feels awkward. But I guess that's okay.

I'm tired. Wish I could go back to bed. But I'm here, writing. That's something, right?

As the week progressed, Alex experimented with different times and places to write. He tried journaling in the evening but found his mind too cluttered from the day. Early mornings worked better - his thoughts were clearer and less influenced by the day's events.

Tip: There's no "perfect" time to journal. Experiment to find what works for you. Some people prefer mornings to set intentions for the day, while others use evening journaling to reflect and unwind.

BUILDING CONSISTENCY

Week 2:

Alex's enthusiasm waned. One morning, he slept through his alarm. Another day, he got distracted by emails. By Friday, he realized he'd only journaled twice that week.

Feeling discouraged, he wrote:

I'm terrible at this. Maybe journaling isn't for me. What's the point if I can't even stick to it for two weeks?

But then he remembered advice he'd read about habit formation. Instead of giving up, he decided to make his goal smaller and more achievable.

Tip: Start small. Consistency matters more than quantity. Even just a few sentences a day can help build the habit.

Alex set a new goal: write for just 5 minutes every day, no matter what. He set a recurring alarm on his phone and left his journal on his nightstand as a visual reminder.

FINDING YOUR VOICE

Week 3:

As journaling became more routine, Alex focused on developing his writing style. He experimented with different approaches:

Monday: Today I'm going to try stream-of-consciousness writing. Just let the thoughts flow without judgment. Work is a stressful deadline coming up not sure if I'll finish in time what if I let everyone down breathe Alex breathe you've got this one step at a time...

Tuesday: Three things I'm grateful for:

1. *The way sunlight filtered through the trees on my morning walk*
2. *The smell of fresh coffee*
3. *An encouraging text from Mom*

Wednesday: Dear Future Self, I hope by the time you read this, you've finished that big project at work. Remember how stressed you were? But you've overcome challenges before, and you'll do it again...

Tip: Your journaling style may evolve over time. Don't be afraid to experiment with different formats and techniques.

OVERCOMING BLOCKS

Week 4:

Alex hit a wall. Staring at the blank page, he felt... blank. No thoughts, no feelings, nothing to write. He scribbled:

I have nothing to say. This is pointless. Maybe I should just give up.

But instead of closing his journal, he decided to write about not knowing what to write. As he described his frustration, other thoughts began to surface. Before he knew it, he'd filled two pages.

Tip: When you feel stuck, write about feeling stuck. Often, the act of writing itself will unlock your thoughts.

REFLECTING ON PROGRESS

One Month Later:

Alex flipped back through his journal, reading entries from the past month. He was surprised to see how his writing had evolved - from hesitant and self-conscious to more open and reflective. He wrote:

It's been a month of journaling. Not every day was easy, but I'm proud I stuck with it. I'm starting to see patterns in my thoughts and behavior. I'm more aware of my emotions. And somehow, putting my worries on paper makes them feel more manageable. I'm curious to see where this journey takes me next.

Research supports Alex's experience. A 2018 study published in the Journal of Medical Internet Research found that regular journaling was associated with decreased mental distress and increased well-being. The key is consistency - participants who wrote more often saw greater benefits.

MAKING IT YOUR OWN

Remember, there's no one "right" way to journal. As you develop your practice, consider these ideas to make journaling work for you:

1. **Create a ritual**: Light a candle, play soft music, or make a cup of tea before you write. This can help signal to your brain that it's time to reflect.
2. **Use prompts**: On days when you're not sure what to write about, use prompts to spark ideas. Websites like "Journal Buddies" offer hundreds of free prompts for all ages.

3. **Mix it up**: Incorporate drawings, collages, or even voice recordings into your journaling practice. A 2016 study in the Journal of the American Art Therapy Association found that creative activities can reduce stress levels.
4. **Review and reflect**: Occasionally re-read your old entries. You might gain new insights or see how far you've come.
5. **Be kind to yourself**: There will be days when you don't feel like writing, and that's okay. The goal is progress, not perfection.

As you embark on your own journaling journey, remember Alex's experience. There may be challenges along the way, but with patience and persistence, you can develop a journaling practice that's meaningful and sustainable for you.

FIVE
THE ART OF REFLECTION

Zoe slumped onto her couch, exhausted after a long day at work. The setting sun cast long shadows across her living room, mirroring the dark thoughts swirling in her mind. She reached for her journal, a habit she'd cultivated over the past few months. As she opened to a fresh page, she paused, pen hovering over the paper.

"What am I even doing?" she wondered aloud. "Am I just venting, or is there more to this?"

Reflective journaling is more than just recounting your day. It's about diving deeper, asking questions, and uncovering insights. Let's peek into Zoe's journal as she explores this technique:

"Today was rough. That project deadline is looming, and I snapped at Tim during our team meeting. I feel terrible about it. Why did I react that way? I guess I'm feeling overwhelmed and... scared. Scared of failing, of letting the team down. But taking it out on Tim isn't fair or helpful. How can I handle this stress better? Maybe I need to talk to my manager about redistributing some tasks..."

As Zoe wrote, she found herself moving from simply describing events to analyzing her reactions and brainstorming solutions. This is the power of reflective journaling.

TECHNIQUES FOR DEEPER REFLECTION

1. The 5 Whys

Zoe decided to dig deeper into her reaction at the meeting. She'd heard about the "5 Whys" technique and decided to give it a try:

Why did I snap at Tim?
Because I felt frustrated.
Why did I feel frustrated?
Because I'm worried about the project deadline.
Why am I worried about the deadline?
Because I'm not sure if we can finish in time.
Why am I not sure if we can finish in time?
Because I've taken on too much responsibility.
Why have I taken on too much responsibility?
Because I'm afraid of appearing incapable or letting the team down.

Zoe sat back, surprised. She hadn't realized how much her fear of appearing incapable was driving her behavior.

Research Note: The "5 Whys" technique was developed by Sakichi Toyoda for the Toyota Motor Corporation. While originally used for problem-solving in manufacturing, it has been adapted for personal development and reflective practices. A 2019 study in the Journal of Business Research found that the 5 Whys technique can lead to more innovative solutions by encouraging deeper analysis of root causes.

2. Perspective Shift

The next day, Zoe decided to try another reflective technique. She wrote about the team meeting incident from Tim's perspective:

"I was explaining my part of the project when Zoe suddenly lashed out at me. It caught me off guard – we work well together. She seemed really stressed. I wonder if she's okay? Maybe she's feeling overwhelmed with the project. I should check in with her, and see if there's any way I can help."

Writing from Tim's point of view helped Zoe see the situation from a new perspective. She realized her behavior might have impacted her colleagues more than she had thought.

3. Future Self

Inspired by her new insights, Zoe decided to write a letter to her future self:

"Dear Future Zoe,

I hope by the time you read this, you've learned to manage your stress better. Remember today, when you snapped at Tim? I hope you've found ways to communicate your concerns more clearly. Have you learned to delegate more? To ask for help when you need it?

I hope you've realized that your worth isn't tied to your productivity. That making mistakes doesn't make you incapable. That your team is there to support you, not judge you.

Be kind to yourself. You're doing the best you can.

Love,

Present Zoe"

As she sealed the letter in an envelope, dated to be opened in six months, Zoe felt a sense of hope. She was laying the groundwork for her own growth.

THE SCIENCE BEHIND REFLECTION

Dr. James Pennebaker, a pioneer in writing therapy research, found that people who engage in expressive writing about traumatic experiences show improvements in both physical and psychological health. The key, he discovered, was in not just recounting events, but in creating narratives that help make sense of experiences.

A 2018 study published in Frontiers in Psychology found that reflective writing can lead to increased self-awareness and improved emotional regulation. The researchers noted that the act of writing allows individuals to externalize their thoughts and emotions, creating psychological distance that can lead to new perspectives.

INTEGRATING REFLECTION INTO DAILY LIFE

As weeks passed, Zoe found herself integrating reflective practices into her daily routine:

- She started each morning by writing three things she was grateful for, setting a positive tone for the day.
- During her lunch break, she'd jot down any challenges she was facing and brainstorm potential solutions.
- Before bed, she'd reflect on the day, noting what went well and what she'd like to improve.

Zoe noticed changes in her daily life too. She was more patient with her colleagues, better at communicating her needs, and more aware of her emotional triggers. When stress arose, she had the tools to process it in a productive way.

ADVANCED REFLECTION TECHNIQUES

As Zoe's reflective practice deepened, she explored more advanced techniques:

1. **Metaphor Analysis**: She described her emotions or

situations using metaphors, then explored what those metaphors revealed about her perceptions.

2. **Values Clarification**: She often reflected on her core values and how her actions aligned (or didn't) with those values.

3. **Cognitive Restructuring**: When she noticed negative thought patterns, she used her journal to challenge and reframe those thoughts.

4. **Mindfulness Journaling**: She practiced describing her present-moment experiences without judgment, enhancing her overall mindfulness.

THE TRANSFORMATIVE POWER OF REFLECTION

Six months later, Zoe opened the letter she'd written to her future self. As she read, tears welled in her eyes. She had indeed grown, in ways both subtle and profound. Her relationship with Tim and other colleagues had improved. She'd learned to delegate more. Above all, she'd developed a kinder, more compassionate relationship with herself.

Zoe picked up her pen and began to write a new entry:

"Reflection isn't always easy. Sometimes it means facing uncomfortable truths about ourselves. But it's through this process that we grow, that we learn, that we become better versions of ourselves. This journal has become more than just a notebook — it's a mirror, a time machine, a trusted friend. Through these pages, I'm not just recording my life; I'm shaping it."

As you embark on your own journey of reflective journaling, remember Zoe's experience. Be patient with yourself. Be willing to ask tough questions and sit with uncomfortable answers. Trust the process. With time and practice, you'll develop a deeper understanding of yourself and the world around you.

Your journal is waiting. What reflections will you discover on its pages?

SIX
CREATIVITY UNLEASHED

Maya sat cross-legged on her bed, surrounded by a chaos of colored pens, washi tape, and magazine clippings. Her new journal lay open before her, its blank pages both inviting and intimidating. She took a deep breath, closed her eyes, and let her hand hover over her supplies.

"Just pick something," she whispered to herself. "It doesn't have to be perfect."

Her fingers closed around a blue pen. She opened her eyes and began to write:

"I don't know what I'm doing. This is supposed to be 'creative journaling,' but I feel anything but creative right now. What if I mess it up? What if—"

Maya stopped, frowning at the words. This wasn't what she had in mind when she decided to explore creative journaling. She was about to tear out the page when she remembered the advice from the art therapist at last week's workshop: "There are no mistakes in creative journaling, only opportunities."

Inspired, Maya decided to transform her doubtful words into something new. She grabbed a yellow highlighter and began tracing abstract shapes around and through the text, letting her hand move as it pleased. As the shapes emerged, she found herself relaxing, enjoying the simple act of creation without judgment.

VISUAL MAPPING: A WINDOW TO THE MIND

Energized by this small victory, Maya turned to a fresh page. In the center, she wrote "My Perfect Day" and circled it. From there, she let her thoughts flow, jotting down ideas and connecting them with colorful lines:

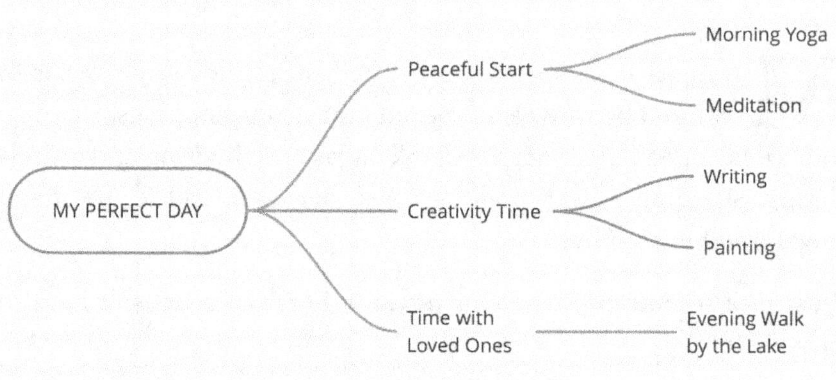

As the map grew, Maya found herself adding small sketches — a sun for a peaceful start, a paintbrush for creativity time, and stick figures for loved ones. The visual representation gave her a new perspective on what truly mattered to her.

"I had no idea I had so many ideas about my perfect day," Maya mused, adding a final flourish to her mind map. "It's like my brain just needed a different way to express itself."

COLLAGE JOURNALING: A DIALOGUE OF IMAGES AND WORDS

The next day, Maya spread out a stack of old magazines on her desk. She flipped through them, tearing out images and words that resonated with her current mood – a stormy sea, a winding path, a bright sunflower, the word "JOURNEY" in bold letters.

As she arranged the pieces on her journal page, a story began to emerge. The stormy sea represented her current uncertainties, the winding path of her journey of self-discovery, and the sunflower her hope for the future. Around these images, she wrote brief reflections:

"The sea of my mind is turbulent now, thoughts crashing like waves. But I'm on a path, winding though it may be. And there, in the distance, a glimmer of sunlight. This journey isn't always easy, but it's mine, and it's beautiful in its own way."

Maya sat back, surprised by the depth of insight that had emerged from this seemingly random collection of images. The collage had given form to feelings she'd struggled to articulate.

ART JOURNALING: WHERE WORDS AND IMAGES DANCE

Inspired by her collage experience, Maya decided to dive deeper into art journaling. She opened her watercolor set, a gift she'd received months ago but had been too intimidated to use.

"No pressure," she reminded herself. "This is about expression, not perfection."

She began by washing the page with soft blues and greens, letting the colors blend and flow. As the paint dried, she saw shapes emerging – were those clouds? Trees? She began to define them with pen, letting her imagination guide her. Alongside the emerging land-scape, a poem began to form in her mind. She wrote it in the sky of her painted world:

"In the space between
thought and expression,
a new world emerges.
Painted in possibility,
written in wonder."

As she added the final touches to her art journal page, Maya felt a sense of accomplishment and joy she hadn't experienced in a long time. This wasn't just journaling — it was a form of self-discovery, a way to access parts of herself she didn't even know existed.

THE SCIENCE OF CREATIVITY

Maya's experiences align with scientific research on the benefits of creative activities:

- A 2016 study published in the Journal of Positive Psychology found that engaging in small creative projects led to increased psychological well-being. Participants reported feeling more enthusiastic and flourishing.
- Neuroscientists have discovered that creative activities can increase the release of dopamine, a neurotransmitter associated with pleasure and motivation. This can lead to a sense of flow and enjoyment.
- Art therapy research has shown that creative expression can help reduce stress and anxiety. A 2016 study in the Journal of the American Art Therapy Association found that 45 minutes of creative activity lessened stress in participants, regardless of artistic experience or talent.

EMBRACING IMPERFECTION: THE HEART OF CREATIVE JOURNALING

As weeks passed, Maya's journal filled with an eclectic mix of writing, drawings, collages, and painted pages. Some days, she produced pages she was proud to share on her Instagram. On other days, her creations felt messy or uninspired. But she kept going, understanding that the value was in the process, not just the outcome.

One evening, leafing through her journal, Maya was struck by how much it reflected her journey – not just in content, but in style. The early pages showed hesitation, with timid lines and cautious colors. As she progressed, the pages became bolder and more experimental. She'd tried techniques that worked well and others that... well, hadn't quite turned out as planned. But each page was a genuine expression of herself.

She turned to a fresh page and wrote:

"This journal is becoming a map of my inner world. It's not always pretty. It's certainly not perfect. But it's real, and it's mine. Through these pages, I'm learning to embrace the messy, beautiful process of creation – and of life itself. I'm learning that creativity isn't about making masterpieces. It's about expression, exploration, and the courage to put something of yourself onto the page."

Maya closed her journal, feeling a deep sense of connection to herself and her creativity. She realized that creative journaling wasn't just about making her journal look pretty – it was a powerful tool for self-expression, emotional processing, and personal growth.

As you embark on your own creative journaling journey, remember Maya's experience. Don't be afraid to experiment, to make "mistakes," to create pages you love and pages you don't. Each mark you make is a step on your creative path.

Your journal is a safe space for exploration. It doesn't judge. It doesn't demand perfection. It simply offers you a place to be your authentic, creative self. So grab your pens, your paints, your glue stick – whatever calls to you. Your next creative discovery awaits.

What will you create today?

SEVEN

THE POWER OF STRUCTURE

Tom stared at his phone, thumb hovering over yet another productivity app. His home screen was a graveyard of abandoned to-do list apps, each promising to be the solution to his chronic disorganization. With a sigh, he tossed the phone aside and reached for the leather-bound notebook his sister had given him for his birthday.

"Bullet journaling," she'd said. "It'll change your life."

Tom flipped open to the first blank page, uncapped his pen, and hesitated. He'd tried journaling before, but it never stuck. Traditional diary entries felt too open-ended, and he struggled to keep track of everything. But as he recalled his sister's enthusiasm, he decided to give it one more shot.

THE INDEX: A MAP FOR YOUR MIND

Tom turned to the first page and wrote "Index" at the top. He'd learned that this was the cornerstone of the bullet journal system, a table of contents that would grow with his journal. As he stared at the blank lines below, he felt a glimmer of hope. Maybe this time, he'd be able to find things in his journal.

FUTURE LOG: PLANTING SEEDS FOR TOMORROW

Next came the Future Log. Tom drew a simple four-page spread, dividing each page into three sections for the upcoming year. As he began jotting down known future events - his cousin's wedding in August, the company retreat in October - he felt a sense of control he hadn't experienced in years. For once, he could see the shape of his year at a glance.

MONTHLY LOG: A BIRD'S EYE VIEW

Turning to a fresh page, Tom created his first Monthly Log for July. On the left page, he wrote out the dates and days of the week in a simple list. On the right, he started a task list for the month. As he transferred items from his various digital apps to this analog system, he realized how much mental clutter he'd been carrying around.

DAILY LOG: WHERE THE RUBBER MEETS THE ROAD

With his broader structure in place, Tom began his first Daily Log. He wrote the date at the top of the page and began listing out his tasks for the day:

- Submit quarterly report
- Call Mom for her birthday
- Pick up dry cleaning
- Schedule dentist appointment

As he wrote, he found himself adding other types of entries:

- \> Team meeting at 2pm

- \- Idea for new project
- * Feeling anxious about the presentation next week

Tom sat back, surprised at how quickly the system was coming together. Each type of entry - tasks, events, notes - had its own signifier, making it easy to distinguish between them at a glance.

COLLECTIONS: CORRALLING SCATTERED THOUGHTS

As days passed, Tom found himself creating special pages for specific topics. He called them Collections, following the bullet journal terminology. He had a page for books he wanted to read, another for workout routines, and one for ideas for his sister's upcoming birthday gift.

One evening, as he was brainstorming for a work project, he created a mind map directly in his journal. The ability to have this creative exploration live alongside his daily tasks and events felt revolutionary.

RAPID LOGGING: THE ART OF CAPTURING QUICKLY

Tom discovered that the real magic of the bullet journal system lay in its speed. Throughout the day, he could quickly jot down tasks, events, or thoughts without needing to decide immediately where they belonged. This "Rapid Logging" technique meant that nothing slipped through the cracks.

During his weekly review, he'd go through these entries, crossing off completed tasks, migrating still-relevant items to new lists, and reflecting on notes and events. This regular review process helped him stay on top of his commitments and gain insights into his productivity patterns.

THE BENEFITS EMERGE

As weeks turned into months, Tom noticed significant changes:

1. **Increased Productivity**: By having all his tasks and notes in one place, Tom felt more in control and focused. He was completing more tasks and feeling less overwhelmed.
2. **Improved Memory**: The act of writing things down by hand seemed to help him remember better. He found himself referring to his journal less often as time went on.
3. **Enhanced Creativity**: The blend of structure and flexibility in his bullet journal allowed for creative thinking alongside practical planning. His problem-solving at work improved as he used his journal for brainstorming and project planning.
4. **Mindfulness**: The ritual of updating his journal each morning and evening brought a sense of mindfulness to his day. He was more aware of how he was spending his time and energy.
5. **Stress Reduction**: As his external organization improved, Tom's mental clutter decreased. He slept better and felt more relaxed.

THE SCIENCE BEHIND THE STRUCTURE

Tom's experiences align with scientific research on the benefits of structured journaling and planning:

- A study published in the Journal of Experimental Psychology found that the act of writing down tasks and goals can increase the likelihood of achieving them. The researchers called this the "intention-behavior gap" - and structured journaling techniques like bullet journaling can help bridge this gap.

- Neuroscientific research has shown that the act of writing by hand engages the brain more deeply than typing, potentially leading to better retention and understanding.
- A 2017 study in the Journal of Management demonstrated that reflective journaling practices (like those incorporated in bullet journaling) can improve work performance and job satisfaction.

EVOLUTION AND PERSONALIZATION

As Tom became more comfortable with the basic bullet journal system, he began to adapt it to his specific needs:

- He created a custom signifier for work-related tasks, helping him quickly identify professional priorities.
- Inspired by habit-tracking layouts he'd seen online, he started a simple tracker for his meditation practice and water intake.
- He experimented with different weekly spread layouts until he found one that perfectly balanced his work and personal commitments.

Six months into his bullet journaling journey, Tom flipped through his now well-worn notebook. Pages filled with tasks, events, notes, and reflections told the story of his days. He smiled as he noticed how his handwriting had become more confident, his layouts more creative, and his reflections more insightful.

On a fresh page, he wrote:

"When I started this journal, I was drowning in disorganization and digital clutter. I was skeptical that a pen and notebook could succeed where countless apps had failed. But this system has become more than just a planner. It's a record of my life, a tool for growth, and a daily practice that grounds me.

I've learned that structure doesn't have to be constricting. In fact, the structure of this journal has given me the freedom to be more creative, more productive, and more present in my life. It's not about rigidly following a system, but about creating a framework that supports my goals and reflects my journey.

Most importantly, I've realized that the power of this journal lies not in its perfect execution, but in the consistent practice of showing up, day after day, to check in with myself and my goals. It's about progress, not perfection."

Tom closed his journal, feeling a deep sense of gratitude for this unexpected tool of transformation. He realized that bullet journaling wasn't just about getting things done – it was a powerful practice for intentional living.

As you embark on your own structured journaling journey, remember Tom's experience. Don't be afraid to experiment, to adapt the system to your needs, to make it truly yours. Your journal is a reflection of your life – let it evolve as you do.

Your next blank page is waiting. What structure will you create to support your dreams and goals?

EIGHT
DIGITAL FRONTIERS

Aisha's fingers hovered over her smartphone screen as the train lurched into motion. Around her, fellow commuters were lost in their devices - scrolling social media, playing games, or staring blankly at news feeds. But Aisha was about to embark on a different kind of digital journey.

She tapped open her journaling app, took a deep breath, and began to type:

"Day 1 of digital journaling. It feels strange not to have pen and paper in hand, but I'm determined to give this a fair shot. The app interface is clean and intuitive. Let's see where this takes me..."

As the cityscape blurred past the window, Aisha dove into her digital journaling adventure, unaware of how it would transform her daily commute - and her life.

MULTI-MEDIA INTEGRATION: CAPTURING LIFE IN FULL COLOR

A week into her experiment, Aisha found herself at her usual spot on the 7:15 train. But today, something was different. The sunrise painted the sky in breathtaking hues of pink and gold. Without missing a beat, she opened her journaling app and snapped a photo.

The app added the location and weather data to her entry. Aisha typed a quick reflection:

"Breathtaking sunrise this morning. It's easy to get caught up in the rush and miss these moments of beauty. Feeling grateful for this reminder to pause and appreciate the world around me."

As she continued writing, Aisha realized how the ability to capture and contextualize moments was adding a new dimension to her journaling practice.

VOICE-TO-TEXT: THOUGHTS AT THE SPEED OF SPEECH

One hectic morning, Aisha found herself running late. As she speed-walked from the train station to her office, a brilliant idea for her current project popped into her head. In the past, she might have lost the thought in the rush of the day. But now, she simply opened her app and tapped the voice-to-text button.

"What if we approached the client presentation as a story, with the data points as plot twists?" she spoke into her phone. The app transcribed her words in real time.

Later that day, Aisha expanded on this seed of an idea, fleshing it out into a full presentation outline. She marveled at how easily she could capture fleeting thoughts and develop them into concrete plans.

PROMPTED JOURNALING: A DAILY DOSE OF INSPIRATION

As Aisha settled into her digital journaling routine, she discovered the app's daily prompt feature. One morning, she was greeted with the question: "What's a small win you've had recently?"

She paused, reflecting on the past week. Then she began to type:

"Yesterday, I finally spoke up in the team meeting about my concerns with the project timeline. It was nerve-wracking, but my manager thanked me for bringing it up. It made me realize I should trust my instincts more and not be afraid to voice my opinions."

This simple prompt led Aisha to recognize and celebrate a moment of personal growth she might have otherwise overlooked.

MOOD TRACKING: PATTERNS IN THE DATA

A month into her digital journaling journey, Aisha noticed the app's mood-tracking feature. Intrigued, she began logging her mood each day with a few quick taps.

As weeks passed, patterns emerged. The app generated a colorful graph of her emotional landscape. Aisha noticed that her mood dipped consistently on Wednesday afternoons and peaked on Saturday mornings. This insight led her to make some changes:

"Realized I've been scheduling all my challenging tasks for Wednesday afternoons. No wonder I've been feeling overwhelmed! Going to try spreading them out through the week and see if it helps."

AI-ASSISTED INSIGHTS: A DIGITAL MIRROR

Three months in, Aisha was surprised by a notification from her journaling app. It had used natural language processing to analyze her entries and offered some insights:

"You frequently mention feeling 'stuck' or 'overwhelmed' when writing about work. However, entries about your photography hobby are consistently positive. Have you considered ways to bring more creativity into your work life?"

Aisha leaned back, startled by the app's perceptiveness. She hadn't noticed this pattern herself, but now that it was pointed out, it resonated deeply. This sparked a series of reflections on her career path and how she might integrate her passion for creativity into her professional life.

THE DIGITAL DILEMMA: NAVIGATING PRIVACY CONCERNS

As Aisha's digital journal filled with personal reflections, cherished memories, and private thoughts, a new concern arose: privacy. One evening, she found herself researching the app's security features and data policies.

She was relieved to find that the app used end-to-end encryption, meaning her entries were scrambled into unreadable code during transmission and storage. Only her personal device held the key to unlock and read the entries.

Still, Aisha took additional precautions:

1. She enabled two-factor authentication for an extra layer of security.
2. She backed up her journal entries to a personal, encrypted hard drive.
3. She was mindful about which entries she synced to the cloud, keeping her most private reflections local to her device.

Aisha made a note in her journal:

"Feeling more secure about my digital journaling setup now. It's a good reminder that in the digital age, we need to be proactive about protecting our personal data. But with the right precautions, the benefits of digital journaling are worth it."

BRIDGING ANALOG AND DIGITAL: THE BEST OF BOTH WORLDS

Six months into her digital journaling journey, Aisha found herself in an unexpected place - an art supply store, admiring a display of well-bound notebooks and sleek pens.

She realized that while digital journaling had become an integral part of her daily routine, she missed the tactile experience of putting pen to paper. That evening, she made an entry in her app:

"Digital journaling has transformed my practice in ways I never expected. The convenience, the multimedia integration, the insights from data analysis - it's all incredibly valuable. But I'm feeling drawn back to paper journaling too. Maybe it doesn't have to be either/or. What if I could combine both?"

Over the next few weeks, Aisha experimented with a hybrid approach:

- She used her app for daily check-ins, quick notes, and photo journals.
- She dedicated time each weekend for long-form reflective writing in a physical journal.
- She would sometimes handwrite entries, take a photo, and add them to her digital journal for easy reference and searchability.

This blended method allowed her to enjoy the best of both worlds - the convenience and features of digital journaling, and the mindful, tactile experience of writing by hand.

THE SCIENCE OF DIGITAL JOURNALING

Aisha's experiences align with emerging research on digital journaling and mental health apps:

- A 2021 study in the Journal of Medical Internet Research found that digital journaling apps can be effective tools for mental health support, particularly when they incorporate features like mood tracking and guided prompts.
- Research published in the journal Computers in Human Behavior demonstrated that multimedia journaling (incorporating photos, videos, and audio) can enhance memory recall and emotional processing compared to text-only journals.
- A study in the Journal of Behavioral Addictions highlighted the importance of mindful engagement with digital tools, suggesting that intentional use of apps (like digital journaling) could counteract some of the negative effects associated with excessive smartphone use.

A NEW CHAPTER IN AN ANCIENT PRACTICE

As Aisha reflected on her digital journaling journey, she realized how much her practice had evolved. What started as a simple experiment has become a powerful tool for self-discovery, productivity, and personal growth.

In her final entry of the year, Aisha wrote:

"When I first started this digital journaling experiment, I worried that technology might create a barrier between me and my thoughts. Instead, it's opened up new ways of understanding myself and my world. I've captured moments I would have missed, recognized patterns I might have overlooked, and found flexibility in my practice that fits my busy life.

But more than the features or the convenience, what I've really gained is a deeper commitment to showing up for myself every day. Whether it's tapping on a screen or putting pen to paper, the real power of journaling - digital or otherwise - lies in the consistent practice of self-reflection and growth.

As we stand on this digital frontier, I'm excited to see how journaling will continue to evolve. But at its core, it remains what it's always been: a conversation with ourselves, a record of our journey, and a tool for becoming who we want to be."

As you embark on your own digital journaling journey, remember Aisha's experience. Embrace the unique features digital platforms can offer, but don't be afraid to blend them with traditional methods if that feels right for you. Be mindful of privacy and security, and always prioritize what helps you maintain a consistent, meaningful practice.

The digital frontier of journaling is vast and ever-expanding. What new terrain will you explore in your practice?

NINE

MINDFULNESS ON THE PAGE

David's alarm chirped, rousing him from sleep. He reached for his phone, thumb hovering over the snooze button as it had countless mornings before. But today was different. Instead of nine more minutes of restless dozing, he swung his feet to the floor, padding to the small desk by the window.

Soft pre-dawn light filtered through the curtains as David settled into his chair. He closed his eyes, taking a deep breath. The world fell away as he focused on the sensation of the pen in his hand, the texture of the paper beneath his fingers. As he exhaled, he began to write, letting his awareness guide his words.

THE SENSORY CHECK-IN: AWAKENING TO THE PRESENT MOMENT

David started his practice by noting what he could perceive with each of his senses:

"I see: The pale blue light of dawn creeping around the edges of the curtains.

I hear: The quiet hum of the refrigerator, a distant dog barking.
I smell: The lingering aroma of last night's herbal tea.
I taste: The faint mintiness of toothpaste.
I feel: The cool smoothness of the pen, the slight chill in the air on my skin."

As he wrote, David found himself noticing details he might have otherwise overlooked - the intricate pattern of wood grain on his desk, the varying pitches in the bird songs outside. This simple exercise grounded him in the present moment, setting a tone of awareness for the day ahead.

THE BODY SCAN: LISTENING TO THE WISDOM OF THE BODY

On another morning, David decided to try a different approach. Moving his attention slowly from his toes to the top of his head, he wrote about any sensations he noticed:

"Toes feel cool against the wooden floor. Slight tension in my calves - maybe from yesterday's run? My stomach feels a bit uneasy - nervous about the presentation later. Shoulders hunched--relaxing them now. Jaw clenched - taking a moment to release that tension."

This practice helped David become more aware of physical sensations and the emotions they might be linked to. He realized how much tension he had been carrying without even noticing. By bringing awareness to these physical states, he found he could start to release them, leading to a sense of greater ease in his body.

THOUGHT OBSERVATION: WATCHING THE MIND'S MOVIE

One morning, when his mind felt especially buzzy, David tried a thought observation exercise. Without judging or trying to change them, he simply noted the thoughts passing through his mind:

"Planning what to wear to work... Worried about that email I forgot to send... Remembering the fun dinner with friends last night... Anxious about the dentist appointment next week... Excited about the upcoming vacation..."

As he wrote, David noticed how quickly his thoughts jumped from one topic to another, often with no logical connection. This exercise helped him recognize thought patterns and practice non-attachment. He realized that he didn't have to believe or act on every thought that crossed his mind.

THE GRATITUDE FLOW: CULTIVATING APPRECIATION

On a day when he was feeling a bit down, David decided to try a gratitude flow. He let his pen move for five minutes, listing everything he felt grateful for, no matter how small:

"Grateful for the warm sun on my face this morning, for the delicious coffee in my favorite mug, for the text from Mom yesterday, for the comfortable shoes I'm wearing, for the colleague who helped me with that tricky project, for the beautiful sunset I saw on my way home..."

As he wrote, David felt his mood lifting. The practice shifted his perspective, helping him focus on the abundance in his life rather than what was lacking.

LOVING-KINDNESS JOURNALING: EXPANDING THE CIRCLE OF COMPASSION

Inspired by the Buddhist metta meditation, David experimented with loving-kindness journaling. He wrote messages of goodwill - first to himself, then to loved ones, acquaintances, difficult people, and extending to all beings:

"May I be happy, healthy, and at peace.

> *May my partner be happy, healthy, and at peace.*
> *May my challenging coworker be happy, healthy, and at peace.*
> *May all beings everywhere be happy, healthy, and at peace."*

As he wrote these words, David felt a warmth spreading through his chest. The practice cultivated a sense of connection and compassion, softening his heart towards himself and others.

THE SCIENCE OF MINDFUL JOURNALING

David's experiences align with scientific research on the benefits of mindfulness and journaling:

- A 2018 study published in the Journal of Clinical Psychology found that a mindfulness-based journaling intervention led to significant reductions in anxiety and increased mindfulness and self-compassion among participants.
- Neuroscientific research has shown that mindfulness practices can lead to changes in the brain associated with improved emotional regulation, attention, and body awareness. A 2011 study published in Psychiatry Research: Neuroimaging found that participation in an 8-week mindfulness program was associated with changes in gray matter concentration in brain regions involved in learning and memory processes, emotion regulation, self-referential processing, and perspective taking.
- A 2020 study in the journal Stress and Health found that gratitude journaling was associated with reduced stress and improved well-being, with effects lasting beyond the intervention period.

CHALLENGES AND GROWTH

As weeks passed, David found his mindful journaling practice evolving. Some days, the words poured out. On other days, he struggled to stay present, his mind constantly wandering to his to-do list or replay of yesterday's conversations.

One frustrating morning, he wrote:

"This is hard today. My mind keeps drifting. I'm judging myself for not being 'mindful enough.' But wait - isn't noticing this also a form of mindfulness? Maybe the struggle is part of the practice too."

This realization was a turning point. David began to approach his practice with more self-compassion, understanding that mindfulness wasn't about achieving a perfect state of calm, but about cultivating awareness of whatever was present - including difficulty and resistance.

INTEGRATION AND TRANSFORMATION

As David's mindful journaling practice deepened, he noticed changes rippling out into his daily life:

- He found himself pausing to take conscious breaths during stressful moments at work, grounding himself in the present moment.
- His conversations became more meaningful as he practiced listening, bringing the same quality of presence to his interactions that he brought to his journaling.
- He became more attuned to his body's signals, addressing tension or discomfort before it became overwhelming.
- His general sense of well-being improved, with greater resilience in the face of life's inevitable challenges.

Six months into his practice, David wrote a reflection:

"When I started this mindful journaling journey, I thought it was about achieving some special state of calm or insight. Now I realize it's simpler - and more profound - than that. It's about showing up, day after day, and paying attention to what's happening in this moment.

Sometimes that moment is peaceful, sometimes it's chaotic. Sometimes my mind is clear, sometimes it's clouded with worry or confusion. But by bringing awareness to whatever is present, I'm learning to meet each moment - and myself - with more acceptance and compassion.

This practice is teaching me that mindfulness isn't just something I do on the page for a few minutes each morning. It's a way of approaching life - with openness, curiosity, and presence. The journal is just the beginning."

As David closed his journal, he felt a sense of calm and clarity. The challenges of his day were still there, but he felt better equipped to face them with presence and equanimity.

As you embark on your own mindful journaling journey, remember David's experience. Be patient with yourself. Embrace both the ease and the difficulty. Trust that each time you show up on the page intending to be present, you're strengthening your capacity for mindfulness in all areas of your life.

Your journal is waiting to be a companion on this journey of awareness. What will you discover in the present moment today?

TEN
JOURNALING FOR PERSONAL DEVELOPMENT

Sophia stared at the glowing "Employee of the Month" plaque on her desk, feeling a strange mix of pride and emptiness. She should be thrilled, but something felt off. With a sigh, she reached for the leather-bound journal she'd started keeping a few months ago. As she opened to a fresh page, she wondered if the answers she sought might be found within its pages.

REFLECTING ON THE JOURNEY: UNCOVERING PATTERNS

Sophia began to write, her pen flying across the page:

"Another 'achievement' to add to the list. But why doesn't it feel like enough? I've been chasing these external markers of success, but I'm still not satisfied. What am I really looking for?"

As she wrote, Sophia found herself flipping back through earlier entries. A pattern began to emerge:

March 15: "Landed the Johnson account. The team seemed impressed, but I feel like a fraud."

April 2: "Gave the presentation to the board. They loved it, but I was a nervous wreck the whole time."
May 20: "Got the promotion. Should be excited, but I'm terrified I won't live up to expectations."

Sophia sat back, a realization dawning. Her pursuit of achievement wasn't bringing her joy; it was feeding a cycle of anxiety and self-doubt. This insight, born from the pages of her journal, was the first step on a new path of self-discovery.

GOAL SETTING: ALIGNING ASPIRATIONS WITH VALUES

Determined to make a change, Sophia decided to use her journal for intentional goal-setting. But this time, instead of focusing on career milestones alone, she started with a different question: "What truly matters to me?"

She created a mind map in her journal, branching out from the central question:

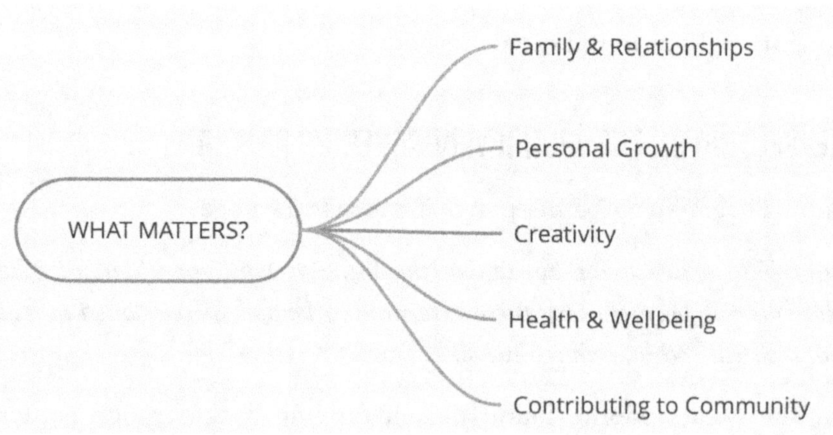

From this foundation, Sophia began to set goals that aligned with her values:

1. Spend quality time with family at least twice a week
2. earn a new skill unrelated to work (pottery class?)
3. Dedicate 30 minutes daily to creative writing
4. Establish a consistent exercise routine
5. Volunteer at the local community garden monthly

As she wrote out these goals, Sophia felt a spark of excitement she hadn't experienced in years. These weren't just tasks to tick off; they were stepping stones to a more fulfilling life.

TRACKING PROGRESS: THE POWER OF SMALL WINS

Inspired by her new direction, Sophia created a simple tracking system in her journal. Each week, she would reflect on her progress toward her goals:

"Week 1:

- *Had dinner with parents on Tuesday, game night with siblings on Saturday. Laughed more than I have in months.*
- *Signed up for pottery class starting next week.*
- *Wrote for 20 minutes 3 out of 7 days. Small start, but it's something.*
- *Went for a run twice. Felt great afterward.*
- *Researched local community gardens. Planning to visit next weekend."*

As weeks passed, Sophia found herself looking forward to these check-ins. Celebrating small wins boosted her motivation, and noticing areas of struggle allowed her to adjust her approach compassionately.

OVERCOMING OBSTACLES: JOURNALING THROUGH CHALLENGES

Not every week was smooth sailing. One evening, after a grueling day at work, Sophia found herself writing:

"Missed pottery class again. Too tired from the Anderson project. Starting to wonder if I can balance all of this. Maybe I should just focus on work. At least I know I'm good at that."

But instead of giving up, Sophia used her journal to problem-solve:

"Obstacles:

1. *Work demands unpredictable*
2. *Often too tired in the evenings*
3. *Feeling guilty about taking time for myself*

Possible solutions:

1. *Set clearer boundaries at work. Learn to say no.*
2. *Try morning workouts/writing sessions.*
3. *Remind myself: that self-care isn't selfish. It makes me better in all areas of life."*

This process of identifying obstacles and brainstorming solutions helped Sophia stay committed to her goals, even when the path was challenging.

CULTIVATING SELF-COMPASSION: REWRITING INNER NARRATIVES

As Sophia continued her journaling practice, she became more aware of her inner critic. One day, she decided to try a new exercise: dialogue with herself. She wrote out a conversation between her inner critic and a kinder, more compassionate inner voice:

"Inner Critic: You're falling behind at work because of all this 'personal development' nonsense. You're going to lose everything you've worked for."

"Compassionate Self: It's natural to feel scared when making big changes. But remember why you started this journey. You were successful but unfulfilled. Now, you're learning to define success on your own terms. It's okay if the path isn't always smooth. You're growing, and that takes time."

This practice of cultivating a more compassionate inner dialogue with intention began to shift Sophia's self-talk in daily life. She found herself responding to setbacks with more kindness and resilience.

THE SCIENCE OF PERSONAL DEVELOPMENT JOURNALING

Sophia's experiences align with scientific research on the benefits of journaling for personal growth:

- A 2018 study published in the Journal of Experimental Psychology found that setting goals and maintaining written records of progress increases the likelihood of achieving those goals. The researchers attributed this to enhanced motivation and self-regulation.
- Research from the University of Rochester demonstrated that writing about personal values can reduce stress and improve problem-solving abilities, especially in high-pressure situations.
- A 2020 study in the journal "Emotion" found that self-compassion exercises, including writing, led to increased motivation and better emotional resilience in the face of personal failings.

INTEGRATION AND TRANSFORMATION

Six months into her personal development journaling journey, Sophia sat down to reflect on her progress:

"Looking back, I hardly recognize the person I was when I started this journal. I was achieving but not living. Now, I feel more aligned, more whole.

Work is still important, but it's not my entire identity anymore. I'm rediscovering parts of myself I'd neglected for years. The pottery class has awakened a creativity I forgot I had. Volunteering at the garden has connected me to my community in beautiful ways.

Most of all, I'm learning to be kinder to myself. To celebrate progress, not just perfection. To see challenges as opportunities for growth rather than threats to my worth.

This journal has become more than just a record of my days. It's a tool for self-discovery, a sounding board for my dreams, and a companion on this journey of becoming. I'm excited to see where it leads next."

As Sophia closed her journal, she glanced at the "Employee of the Month" plaque. It no longer filled her with that mix of pride and emptiness. Instead, she felt a quiet confidence. She was writing her own definition of success now, one journal entry at a time.

As you embark on your own personal development journaling journey, remember Sophia's experience. Use your journal not just to record your life, but to shape it intentionally. Set goals that align with your values, track your progress, work through obstacles, and cultivate self-compassion.

Your journal is more than a notebook; it's a powerful tool for transformation. What story of growth will you write on its pages?

ELEVEN
EMOTIONAL INTELLIGENCE AND SELF-AWARENESS

Ethan slammed the car door, his hands shaking with anger. Another argument with his partner, another day ruined. As he stomped up to his apartment, he felt a familiar sense of helplessness wash over him. Why did he always react this way? Why couldn't he control his emotions?

With a heavy sigh, Ethan reached for the journal he'd started keeping on his therapist's recommendation. He'd been skeptical at first, but as he opened to a fresh page, he felt a glimmer of hope. Maybe, just maybe, the answers he sought were hidden somewhere in these pages.

IDENTIFYING EMOTIONS: THE FIRST STEP TO UNDERSTANDING

Ethan began to write, his pen flying across the page:

"I'm angry. No, furious. But there's something else too. Underneath the anger, I feel... hurt? Scared? I don't even know. How can I not know what I'm feeling?"

As he wrote, Ethan realized how little attention he usually paid to his emotional state. He was used to broad strokes - happy, sad, angry - but the nuances often escaped him. Determined to change this, he decided to start each journal entry with an emotion check-in.

Over the next few weeks, Ethan's emotional vocabulary expanded:

"Monday: Feeling anxious about the presentation tomorrow, but also a bit excited. There's a flutter in my stomach that could be either.

Wednesday: Disappointed about the project setback, but also relieved that I don't have to rush the deadline. It's an odd mix.

Friday: Frustrated with my partner, but underneath that, I think I'm actually feeling insecure. Worried that I'm not good enough."

This simple practice of naming his emotions was the first step on Ethan's journey to greater emotional intelligence.

IDENTIFYING TRIGGERS: CONNECTING THE DOTS

As Ethan continued his daily journaling practice, he began to notice patterns. Certain situations seemed to consistently trigger strong emotional reactions. He decided to dig deeper:

"Argument Trigger Analysis:
What happened: Partner criticized my choice of restaurant
Initial reaction: Anger, defensiveness
Underlying emotion: Shame, feeling like I can't do anything right
Possible root: Dad's constant criticism when I was growing up?
Work Stress Trigger Analysis:
What happened: Boss asked for project update in the team meeting
Initial reaction: Anxiety, feeling flustered
Underlying emotion: Fear of being exposed as incompetent
Possible root: Imposter syndrome, never feeling good enough"

As Ethan connected his emotional reactions to past experiences and underlying beliefs, he felt a sense of empowerment. He couldn't change his past, but understanding these connections gave him a new perspective on his present reactions.

EMOTION REGULATION: DEVELOPING NEW STRATEGIES

Armed with a better understanding of his emotional landscape, Ethan was ready to work on regulating his reactions. He used his journal to brainstorm and practice new strategies:

"Emotion Regulation Toolkit:

1. *Deep breathing: Count to 4 on inhale, and 6 on exhale. Helps calm the nervous system.*
2. *Reframing: Ask 'What else could this mean?' to challenge initial negative interpretations.*
3. *Time-out: It's okay to say 'I need a moment' and step away to collect my thoughts.*
4. *Reality check: Are my emotions proportionate to the situation? Use a 1-10 scale to assess.*
5. *Self-compassion: Treat myself with kindness. What would I say to a friend in this situation?"*

Ethan practiced these techniques daily, using his journal to reflect on their effectiveness:

"Used the time-out technique during an argument today. Felt weird at first, but it gave me space to calm down and think more clearly. We were actually able to resolve the issue instead of it escalating. Progress!"

DEVELOPING EMPATHY: SEEING BEYOND OURSELVES

As Ethan's emotional intelligence grew, he realized his journey wasn't just about understanding himself better - it was also about understanding others. He decided to incorporate empathy exercises into his journaling practice:

"Empathy Exercise: Partner's Perspective
Situation: The restaurant argument
How might they have felt? Possibly disappointed, unheard, or undervalued?
What might be going on in their life to contribute to this reaction? They've been stressed about work lately, maybe needed a night out to relax.
How could I respond with more empathy next time? Acknowledge their feelings, ask about their preferences before deciding"

These exercises helped Ethan see beyond his own emotional reactions and consider the feelings and perspectives of others. Over time, he found his relationships improving as he became more attuned to the emotional needs of those around him.

EMOTIONAL INTELLIGENCE IN ACTION: REAL-LIFE APPLICATION

Three months into his emotional intelligence journaling journey, Ethan faced a significant test. A major project at work hit an unexpected snag, and his boss called an emergency team meeting. In the past, this situation would have sent Ethan into a tailspin of anxiety and self-doubt. But this time, he paused, took a deep breath, and opened his journal:

Emergency Meeting Emotional Check-in:

Initial emotion: Anxiety (7/10 intensity)

Physical sensations: Tight chest, sweaty palms

Potential triggers: Fear of failure, imposter syndrome

Reframe: This is a challenge, not a disaster. The team is capable. My input is valuable.

Action plan: Take three deep breaths before speaking. Focus on solutions, not blame. It's okay to ask for help or clarification."

Armed with this self-awareness and strategy, Ethan entered the meeting feeling more centered and confident. He contributed to the discussion, even finding the courage to propose an innovative solution. To his surprise, his boss praised his level-headed approach.

That evening, Ethan reflected in his journal:

"I handled today so differently than I would have just a few months ago. Instead of getting lost in my anxiety, I was able to recognize it, regulate it, and still perform effectively. It wasn't perfect - I still felt nervous - but I didn't let that control me. This emotional intelligence stuff really works!"

THE SCIENCE OF EMOTIONAL INTELLIGENCE

Ethan's experiences align with scientific research on emotional intelligence and journaling:

- A 2019 study published in the Journal of Personality and Social Psychology found that people who regularly practice emotional labeling (identifying and naming their emotions) show improved emotion regulation and decreased negative emotional experiences over time.
- Research from Yale University demonstrated that individuals with higher emotional intelligence tend to perform better under pressure and show greater leadership capabilities in the workplace.
- A 2020 meta-analysis in the journal Psychological Bulletin found that interventions designed to increase emotional intelligence, including reflective writing practices, led to significant improvements in both personal and professional outcomes.

INTEGRATION AND TRANSFORMATION

Six months into his emotional intelligence journaling practice, Ethan sat down to reflect on his progress:

"Looking back at my early entries, I'm amazed at how far I've come. I used to feel at the mercy of my emotions, constantly reacting without understanding why. Now, I feel like I have a roadmap to my inner world.

I'm not perfect - I still have moments of emotional turbulence. But now I have the tools to navigate those storms. I can name what I'm feeling, understand where it's coming from, and choose how to respond.

Most importantly, this journey has transformed my relationships. I'm more patient with my partner, more understanding with my colleagues, and kinder to myself. I'm having conversations I never could have had before, building deeper connections, and resolving conflicts more constructively.

This journal has become more than just a record of my emotions. It's a training ground for emotional intelligence, and a safe space to explore and grow. I'm excited to see how much further this practice will take me."

As Ethan closed his journal, he felt a sense of peace he'd rarely experienced before. He was no longer afraid of his emotions or the emotions of others. Instead, he saw them as valuable data, guiding him towards a richer, more authentic life.

As you embark on your own emotional intelligence journaling journey, remember Ethan's experience. Use your journal not just to vent emotions, but to understand them. Practice identifying your feelings, exploring their roots, and developing strategies to regulate them. Cultivate empathy by considering the perspectives of others.

Your journal is more than a diary; it's a powerful tool for developing emotional intelligence. What new insights into your emotional world will you discover on its pages?

TWELVE
JOURNALING FOR CREATIVITY

Lila stared at the blinking cursor on her laptop screen, the blank document a stark reminder of her writer's block. She'd been trying to start her novel for months, but the words wouldn't come. With a frustrated sigh, she closed her laptop and reached for the leather-bound journal her best friend had given her for her birthday.

"When you can't write, write about not being able to write," her friend had said. Lila had scoffed at the time, but now, desperate for any kind of breakthrough, she decided to give it a try.

FREEWRITING: UNLEASHING THE SUBCONSCIOUS

Lila opened to a fresh page and began to write without stopping, letting her thoughts flow onto the paper:

"I can't write I don't know what's wrong with me maybe I'm not a writer after all who am I kidding thinking I could write a novel I should just give up and stick to my day job but I love writing or at least I used to before it became this impossible task maybe if I just..."

She wrote for ten minutes straight, her hand cramping from the unaccustomed exercise. When she stopped and read over what she'd written, she was surprised to find a spark of an idea buried in the stream of consciousness:

"...maybe my protagonist isn't stuck because of the plot maybe she's stuck because she's afraid of success what if that's my problem too..."

This small insight, born from the act of freewriting, was the first crack in Lila's creative dam.

MIND MAPPING: VISUALIZING CONNECTIONS

Energized by this breakthrough, Lila decided to explore her idea further. She turned to a blank page and wrote "FEAR OF SUCCESS" in the center, circling it. From there, she let her mind wander, jotting down related thoughts and connecting them with lines:

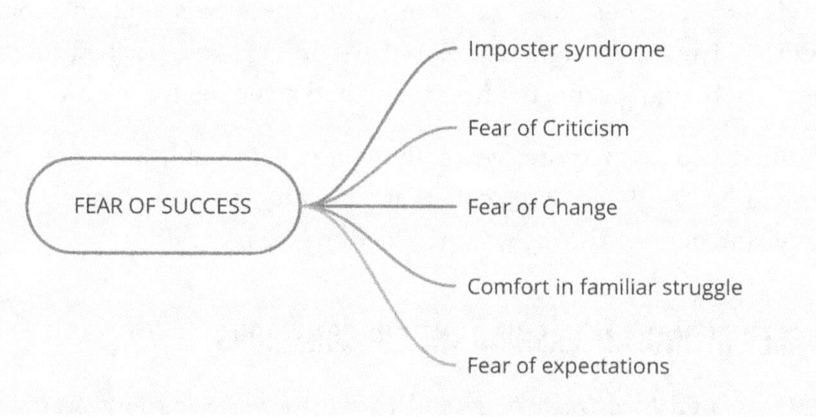

As the mind map grew, Lila saw connections she hadn't noticed before. This visual representation of her thoughts gave her a new perspective on her protagonist's motivations - and her own.

DIALOGUE WITH THE INNER CRITIC: CONFRONTING CREATIVE BLOCKS

Despite her progress, Lila still found herself hesitating to start her novel. She decided to try another journaling technique: dialoguing with her inner critic. She wrote out a conversation between her creative self and the voice of doubt:

> *Creative Self: I'm ready to write this novel. I have ideas, I have the skills.*
> *Inner Critic: But what if it's terrible? What if everyone hates it?*
> *Creative Self: Not everyone will like it, and that's okay. I'm writing for myself first.*
> *Inner Critic: You're wasting your time. You should focus on your real job.*
> *Creative Self: Writing is part of who I am. Even if it never gets published, the act of creation is valuable.*

As she wrote, Lila felt the power of her inner critic diminishing. By giving voice to her fears on the page, she was able to confront and challenge them.

SENSORY EXPLORATION: BRINGING SCENES TO LIFE

With renewed confidence, Lila decided to use her journal to explore the world of her novel. She chose a key scene and wrote a sensory description, focusing on engaging all five senses:

"The old bookstore smelled of leather and dust, with a hint of vanilla from the cafe next door. Sunlight streamed through the stained-glass window, casting colorful patterns on the worn wooden floor. The quiet was broken only by the occasional creak of a floorboard or the soft rustle of turning pages. Sarah ran her fingers along the spines of the books, feeling the

varied textures of cloth, paper, and leather bindings. She could almost taste the stories waiting to be discovered..."

This exercise helped Lila immerse herself in her fictional world, making it feel more real and vibrant. She found herself excited to translate this richness into her novel.

CHARACTER JOURNALING: DEEPENING CHARACTER DEVELOPMENT

To better understand her characters, Lila decided to write journal entries from their perspectives. She started with her protagonist, Sarah:

"Dear Diary,

I stood in front of the 'Employee of the Month' plaque today, seeing my name engraved there, and all I felt was panic. Everyone keeps congratulating me, telling me I'm on the fast track to management. They don't understand that every step up the ladder feels like a step away from my dreams. But how can I tell them that their version of success feels like failure to me? How can I explain that the thought of being trapped in this corporate world for the rest of my life terrifies me more than any risk ever could?

I know I should be grateful. And I am. But there's a voice inside me screaming that there's more to life than this. I'm just not sure I'm brave enough to listen to it."

This exercise gave Lila deep insights into Sarah's internal conflicts, making her character feel more three-dimensional and relatable.

THE SCIENCE OF CREATIVE JOURNALING

Lila's experiences align with scientific research on creativity and writing:

- A 2014 study published in the journal Psychological Science found that handwriting, as opposed to typing, leads to increased neural activity in areas of the brain associated with learning and creativity.
- Research from the University of Texas at Austin demonstrated that expressive writing can help individuals process complex emotions and experiences, which can reduce mental blocks that inhibit creativity.
- A 2019 study in Thinking Skills and Creativity journal showed that regular free writing exercises can improve divergent thinking skills, a key component of creativity.

INTEGRATION AND TRANSFORMATION

Three months into her creative journaling practice, Lila sat down to reflect on her progress:

"When I started this journal, I was creatively blocked and full of self-doubt. Now, I have the first draft of three chapters and a clear roadmap for the rest of my novel.

But more than that, I've rediscovered the joy of writing. These pages have become a playground for my imagination, a safe space to explore ideas without judgment. I've learned that creativity isn't about waiting for inspiration to strike - it's about showing up, day after day, and doing the work.

I've also realized that my creative journey is about more than just writing a novel. It's about self-discovery, about having the courage to express my authentic voice. Every time I open this journal, I'm not just creating a story - I'm creating myself.

The blank page doesn't terrify me anymore. Instead, I see it as an invitation to explore, to play, to create. I can't wait to see what I'll discover next."

As Lila closed her journal and opened her laptop, she felt a sense of excitement she hadn't experienced in years. The cursor still blinked on the blank document, but now, instead of an accusation, it felt like a promise. She placed her fingers on the keyboard and began to write.

As you embark on your own creative journaling journey, remember Lila's experience. Use your journal not just as a receptacle for finished ideas, but as a laboratory for experimentation and growth. Try freewriting to bypass your inner critic, mind mapping to visualize connections and character journaling to deepen your understanding of fictional worlds.

Your journal is more than a notebook; it's a creative incubator, a safe space to nurture your ideas and artistic voice. What new worlds will you create on its pages?

THIRTEEN
PROBLEM-SOLVING AND DECISION MAKING

Alex stared at the two job offers laid out on his kitchen table, feeling paralyzed by indecision. One promised higher pay and prestige, the other better work-life balance and growth opportunities. He'd been weighing the pros and cons for days, but still couldn't make a choice. With a frustrated sigh, he reached for his journal, hoping that putting his thoughts on paper might bring some clarity.

BRAIN DUMP: CLEARING MENTAL CLUTTER

Alex opened to a fresh page and began pouring all his jumbled thoughts onto the paper:

"Can't decide job A more money but longer hours job B less pay but better culture what if I choose wrong what if I regret it what about career growth but what about time for hobbies and relationships parents think I should take job A friends say job B is better for long-term happiness but what if..."

He wrote non-stop for ten minutes, his hand cramping from the effort. When he finally put down his pen and read over what he'd written, he was surprised to see themes emerging that he hadn't consciously considered before. The act of brain dumping had brought subconscious concerns to the surface.

MIND MAPPING: VISUALIZING THE DECISION

Intrigued by the patterns he was seeing, Alex decided to create a mind map of his decision. He drew two large circles, one for each job offer, and began branching out with various factors:

Job A	Job B
Higher Salary	Better Work-Life Balance
Financial security	Time for hobbies
Lifestyle upgrade	Less stress
Prestige	Growth Opportunities
Career advancement	Skill development
Impressive to others	Potential for advancement
Longer Hours	Lower Salary
Less personal time	Budget constraints
Potential burnout	Delayed financial goals

As he connected ideas and added sub-branches, Alex began to see the decision in a new light. The visual representation helped him understand the full impact of each choice.

PROS AND CONS: WEIGHING THE OPTIONS

To dig deeper, Alex decided to create a detailed pros and cons list for each job offer:

"Job A:

Pros:

- Higher salary: Could pay off student loans faster

- Prestigious company: Looks great on resume

- Cutting-edge projects: Working with the latest technology

Cons:

- Long hours: Less time for personal life

- High-stress environment: Potential for burnout

- Limited growth opportunities: Narrow focus on specific tasks

Job B:

Pros:

- Better work-life balance: Time for hobbies and relationships

- Supportive company culture: Emphasis on employee well-being

- Diverse responsibilities: Opportunity to develop broad skill set

Cons:

- Lower salary: Might delay financial goals

- Less prestigious company: Might not impress future employers

- Smaller projects: Potentially less exciting work"

As he reviewed his lists, Alex realized that some factors held more weight for him than others. He decided to add a ranking system, scoring each pro and con on a scale of 1-5 based on its importance to him.

FUTURE SELF VISUALIZATION: LONG-TERM PERSPECTIVE

To gain a different perspective, Alex decided to try a future self-visualization exercise. He wrote two letters, one from his future self having chosen Job A, and another having chosen Job B:

"Dear Present Alex,

It's been five years since you chose Job A. The salary and prestige have been nice, but I'm writing this from a hotel room at 11 PM, having missed another one of Mom's birthday dinners. I'm respected in my field, but I'm exhausted all the time. I can't remember the last time I played guitar or went hiking. I'm successful by society's standards, but I'm not sure I'm happy...

vs.

Dear Present Alex,

It's been five years since you chose Job B. Life looks different than you expected. We're not driving a fancy car, but last weekend we hiked Mount Rainier, something we'd always dreamed of. Work is challenging and fulfilling. I'm learning something new every day. Yesterday, I mentored a new employee and realized how much I've grown. We're not rich, but we're comfortable, and more importantly, we're content..."

As he read over these letters, Alex felt a shift in his perspective. The exercise had brought his personal values into sharper focus.

DECISION MATRIX: QUANTIFYING THE CHOICE

For a more analytical approach, Alex created a decision matrix. He listed the key factors for his decision, assigned each a weight based on importance, and then scored each job on these factors:

Factor	Weight	Job A Score	Job A Weighted	Job B Score	Job B Weighted
Salary	0.3	9	2.7	6	1.8
Work-Life Balance	0.25	4	1	9	2.25
Growth Potential	0.2	6	1.2	8	1.6
Company Culture	0.15	5	0.75	9	1.35
Job Security	0.1	7	0.7	7	0.7
TOTAL	1		6.35		7.7

The matrix provided a numerical perspective on his decision, but Alex realized that the process of creating it was just as valuable as the result. Assigning weights to different factors forced him to consider what mattered most to him.

OVERCOMING ANALYSIS PARALYSIS: TAKING ACTION

Despite all his journaling exercises, Alex still felt hesitant to make a final decision. He recognized that he was falling into analysis paralysis. To break free, he decided to use a technique he'd read about setting a decision deadline.

He wrote in his journal:

"I hereby commit to making a final decision by 5 PM this Friday. Until then, I will continue to reflect and gather any additional information I need. But at 5 PM, I will choose, trusting that I've done my due diligence and that I can handle whatever consequences come."

Setting this deadline lifted a weight off Alex's shoulders. He had permitted himself to stop endlessly deliberating and to move forward.

INTEGRATION AND ACTION

As the decision deadline approached, Alex reviewed all his journal entries related to this choice. He was surprised to find that the answer had been emerging through his writing. The various exercises helped him clarify his priorities and values.

At 4:55 PM on Friday, he made his final journal entry on the topic:

"After careful consideration, I've decided to accept Job B. While the lower salary is a drawback, the opportunity for growth, better work-life balance, and alignment with my personal values make it the right choice for me at this stage in my life. I feel a sense of peace with this decision that I hadn't

expected. The journaling process has helped me understand myself better and trust my own judgment.

More than just solving this particular problem, I've learned a new approach to decision-making. Breaking down the problem, examining it from different angles, and connecting with my values through writing has been invaluable. I plan to use these techniques for future decisions, big and small.

I'm grateful for this journal. It's been more than just a sounding board – it's been a tool for clarity, a catalyst for self-discovery, and ultimately, a pathway to decisive action."

Alex closed his journal, picked up his phone, and dialed the number for Job B. As he accepted the offer, he felt a sense of confidence and excitement about the future. He knew challenges lay ahead, but he also knew he had the tools to face them.

As you face your own decisions and problems, remember Alex's journey. Your journal can be more than a record of your thoughts – it can be an active tool for problem-solving and decision-making. Try brain dumping to clear mental clutter, mind mapping to visualize connections, pros and cons lists to weigh options, future self-visualization to gain perspective, and decision matrices to quantify choices.

Remember, the goal isn't just to solve a single problem, but to develop a personalized toolkit for approaching life's challenges. What decision will you unravel in your journal pages today?

FOURTEEN
JOURNALING FOR
SPECIFIC LIFE SITUATIONS

COPING WITH GRIEF: SARAH'S STORY

Sarah's trembling hand hovered over the blank page of her new journal. The leather cover still smelled new, a gift from her sister "to help with the process," whatever that meant. How could writing ease the gaping hole left by her mother's sudden passing?

With a deep breath, she began:

"Mom, it's been a week since you left us. I don't know how to do this without you..."

Her vision blurred as tears splattered onto the page, smearing the ink. But she kept writing, pouring out her pain, anger, and confusion. As the words flowed, something shifted. The ache in her chest didn't disappear, but it felt... contained, somehow. As if putting her grief on paper gave it shape, and made it manageable.

Over the following weeks, Sarah developed a ritual. Each morning, she'd write a letter to her mother:

"Remember that recipe for apple pie you always promised to teach me? I tried to make it yesterday. It was a disaster, but it made me laugh imagining what you'd say. Probably something like, 'Honey, baking is an art. You just need practice... and maybe a fire extinguisher.'"

Some days, the entries were tear-stained laments. Other days, cherished memories or simple updates about daily life. Through her journal, Sarah found a way to continue her relationship with her mother, processing her loss one page at a time.

MANAGING CHRONIC ILLNESS: JAMES' JOURNEY

James glared at the pill organizer on his nightstand, a plastic reminder of the rheumatoid arthritis that had derailed his life six months ago. His doctor had suggested keeping a symptom journal, but it felt like admitting defeat. Still, with a resigned sigh, he opened the notebook:

"Pain level: 7/10. Joints feel like they're filled with ground glass. Fatigue is bad today. Missed Lisa's recital. Again. Starting to wonder if this is my new normal."

As days passed, James found himself noting not just symptoms, but other aspects of his life:

"Tried that new Mediterranean diet. Pain seems a bit better? Hard to tell. But the recipes are actually pretty good. Bonus: cooking gives me something to do on bad days."

" Finally told my boss about the RA. Was terrified, but he was understanding. We're going to try a flexible work arrangement. Feeling cautiously optimistic."

To his surprise, the journal became more than just a log of his illness. It became a tool for tracking patterns, celebrating small victories, and finding ways to adapt to his new reality.

During his next doctor's appointment, James brought his journal. Together, they identified triggers and treatment effects he hadn't noticed. For the first time since his diagnosis, James felt a sense of control.

NAVIGATING CAREER TRANSITIONS: ELENA'S EXPEDITION

Elena stared at her resignation letter, heart pounding. After ten years in finance, she was leaving to pursue her dream of opening a bakery. Exciting? Yes. Terrifying? Absolutely.

She flipped open her journal, a constant companion through many life changes:

"It's done. I handed in my resignation. I thought I'd feel elated, but mostly I'm panicking. What if I'm making a huge mistake?"

Elena had learned the power of journaling through previous challenges. Now, she used it to navigate this massive life transition:

Mind Mapping: She created a sprawling mind map of her new venture, branches spreading across two pages: "Menu Ideas," "Marketing Strategies," "Funding Options," and "Skills to Develop."

Fear-Setting: Inspired by Tim Ferriss, she confronted her worries head-on:

"Worst case scenarios:

1. Bakery fails, I lose all my savings

- *Could I recover? Yes, would be hard but not impossible. Could return to finance for a time.*

2. I realize I hate running a business

- *Learning experience. Could sell or hire a manager.*

3. I miss the stability of my old job

- *Reminder: I was miserable. Growth requires discomfort."*

Skills Inventory: Elena listed all the abilities she'd developed in her finance career, then brainstormed how each could apply to running a bakery. She was surprised by how transferable many skills were.

Visualization: She wrote a detailed description of her ideal day as a bakery owner, from the smell of fresh bread to the smiles on customers' faces. This vision became her north star on tough days.

As weeks passed, her journal entries evolved from panic to problem-solving:

"Met with the small business advisor today. Next steps: finalize business plan, scout locations, take that food safety certification course."

"Recipe testing day! Note to self: less sugar in the lemon bars, more vanilla in the chocolate cake."

Through her journal, Elena not only documented her journey but shaped it, turning vague dreams into concrete plans.

JOURNALING FOR PERSONAL GROWTH: MIGUEL'S METAMORPHOSIS

Miguel slouched in his chair, the words of his recent performance review echoing in his mind: "Lacks initiative... Struggles with team collaboration... Resistant to feedback." He'd been passed over for promotion again, and the frustration was reaching a boiling point.

With a mix of anger and determination, he opened a new notebook:

"I'm tired of feeling stuck. Something needs to change, and I guess that something is me. But how?"

Thus began Miguel's journey of personal development, with his journal as both a mirror and roadmap:

Self-Reflection: Miguel started with brutal honesty, examining the feedback he'd received:

"Do I really resist feedback? Initial reaction: No! But... thinking back to that project with Sarah. Did I get defensive when she suggested changes? Maybe I need to work on receiving criticism more openly."

Goal Setting: He used the SMART framework to set concrete goals:

"By the end of this quarter:

- Volunteer to lead at least one team project

- Ask for feedback from colleagues after each major task

- Attend 2 networking events to expand my professional circle"

Habit Tracking: Miguel created a simple chart to monitor his progress on key behaviors:

Week 1	M	T	W	Th	F
Active Listening	X	X	-	X	X
Offer Help to Collegue	X	-	X	-	X
Professional Development	-	X	-	-	X

Gratitude Practice: To combat his tendency towards negativity, Miguel ended each entry with three things he was grateful for at work:

"1. John's patience in explaining the new software

2. The challenge of the Anderson project - stretching my skills

3. Free bagels in the breakroom (seriously, they make Mondays bearable)"

Reflection and Iteration: Every month, Miguel reviewed his progress, adjusting his approach as needed:

"Insight: I'm more likely to speak up in meetings when I've prepared

talking points beforehand. New habit to develop: Spend 10 minutes prepping before each meeting."

As weeks turned to months, Miguel's journal became a record of his transformation. Over time entries shifted from frustration to pride in his growth:

"Led the team presentation today. Nervous as hell, but it went well. Sarah actually complimented my openness to the team's input. A year ago, I would've tried to do it all myself. Progress!"

Through consistent journaling, Miguel not only improved his performance at work but developed greater self-awareness and confidence that spilled into all areas of his life.

THE SCIENCE BEHIND SITUATIONAL JOURNALING

Research supports the effectiveness of journaling in various life situations:

- A 2018 study in the journal Death Studies found that expressive writing can reduce symptoms of complicated grief.
- Research published in Pain Medicine in 2019 showed that pain journaling can improve pain management and quality of life for chronic pain patients.
- A longitudinal study in the Journal of Applied Psychology demonstrated that reflective journaling during career transitions leads to higher job satisfaction and performance in new roles.
- A 2020 meta-analysis in Frontiers in Psychology found that gratitude journaling is associated with increased well-being and reduced symptoms of depression and anxiety.

INTEGRATING JOURNALING INTO YOUR LIFE

As you face your own life challenges, remember the journeys of Sarah, James, Elena, and Miguel. Your journal can be more than a diary; it's a tool for coping, understanding, planning, and growing.

Whether you're navigating grief, managing health issues, making a career change, or working on personal development, consider how journaling might support you:

1. Choose a journaling method that resonates with your situation and personality.
2. Set a regular time for journaling, even if it's just a few minutes a day.
3. Be honest in your writing – your journal is for you, not for an audience.
4. Experiment with different techniques: free writing, structured prompts, mind mapping, and goal-setting.
5. Review your entries from time to time to track patterns and progress.
6. Be patient with yourself. Growth and healing take time, and your journal is a companion on that journey.

Remember, there's no "right" way to journal. The most powerful practice is the one you can maintain over time. Your journal is waiting to help you navigate life's challenges. What page will you write today?

FIFTEEN
TRAVEL AND NATURE JOURNALING

The crisp mountain air filled Olivia's lungs as she reached the summit, her legs trembling from the steep climb. Lowering her backpack, she pulled out a well-worn leather journal and a set of watercolor pencils. The vast landscape before her begged to be captured, not just in memory, but on paper.

THE ART OF OBSERVATION: ZOE'S URBAN SKETCHING ADVENTURE

Meanwhile, in the heart of bustling Tokyo, Zoe sat at a small cafe, her sketchbook open on the table. The steam from her matcha latte curled upwards as she observed the scene before her. A group of schoolgirls in crisp uniforms giggled as they passed, their laughter mixing with the rhythmic chime of a nearby temple bell.

Zoe's pen moved across the page, capturing not just the visual details, but the essence of the moment:

"Tokyo, Shibuya Crossing, 2 PM:

Organized chaos. Hundreds of people, a human tide held back by traffic lights. When the signal changes, they surge forward in a breathtaking dance of near-misses and polite bows. The air thrums with energy and the scent of yakitori from a nearby stand."

Next to her quick sketch of the crossing, Zoe pasted a train ticket and a colorful candy wrapper, adding texture and memory to the page.

TECHNIQUES FOR CAPTURING THE MOMENT

As Olivia settled into her journaling spot atop the mountain, she remembered the techniques she'd developed over years of travel:

1. Quick Gesture Sketches: She began with rapid, loose lines capturing the basic shapes of the mountains. These weren't meant to be perfect but to train her eye and warm up her hand.

2. Color Notes: Next to her sketch, she jotted down color observations:

- *"Sky: Deep cerulean fading to pale azure at the horizon*
- *Distant peaks: Layered purples, each range lighter than the last*
- *Foreground: Sun-bleached grasses, golden in the late afternoon light"*

3. Sensory Details: Closing her eyes, Olivia focused on her other senses:

- *"Sound: Wind whistling through rocky crags, the distant cry of an eagle*
- *Smell: Pine resin, sun-warmed stone, a hint of snow from higher elevations*
- *Touch: Rough granite beneath my palms, cool breeze on sun-warmed skin"*

4. Watercolor Washes: With her observations complete, Olivia began adding soft washes of color to her sketch, letting the pigments blend and flow, mirroring the natural beauty before her.

OVERCOMING CHALLENGES: ALEX'S RAINFOREST EXPEDITION

Deep in the Amazon rainforest, Alex swatted at mosquitoes as he tried to sketch a vibrant toucan perched high in the canopy. The humidity made his paper buckle, and the constant motion of the forest made it difficult to focus on any one thing for long.

Frustrated, he turned to a new page and decided to embrace the chaos:

"June 15, Amazon Rainforest:

Everything here is alive and in constant motion. Trying to capture a single moment feels like trying to hold water in my hands. Instead, impressions:

- *Dappled light filtering through layers of leaves*
- *A cacophony of sounds: bird calls, insect buzzes, the distant roar of a howler monkey*
- *The earthy scent of decomposition and new growth, nature's cycle in full force*
- *Flashes of color: a blue morpho butterfly, scarlet macaw feathers, neon-bright tree frogs*

My skin is slick with sweat and bug spray. This place is beautiful and terrifying, nurturing and deadly all at once. I've never felt so alive, or so small."

Next to his written observations, Alex created a collage of quick sketches: leaves of various shapes, the silhouette of a jaguar glimpsed on the riverbank, the intricate pattern of a spider's web glistening with dew.

INTEGRATING TECHNOLOGY: MAYA'S DIGITAL NATURE JOURNAL

As the sun set over the Serengeti, Maya pulled out her tablet. A wildlife photographer by trade, she had initially resisted the idea of digital journaling, preferring the tactile experience of pen and paper. But over time, she'd discovered unique advantages to the digital format.

Using a stylus, Maya quickly sketched the silhouette of an acacia tree against the blazing sky. With a few taps, she added a wash of vibrant oranges and reds, perfectly capturing the intensity of the African sunset.

Next to her sketch, she typed:

"Serengeti, Day 12:

The sky is on fire, painting everything in warm hues. A family of elephants moves slowly across the plain, their dark shapes stark against the fading light. In the distance, a lion's roar ripples through the cooling air. The day's heat radiates from the earth, mixing with the first hints of night's chill.

Earlier, captured incredible shots of a cheetah hunt. The raw power and grace of these animals never cease to amaze me. Video clip attached - the sound of their purring up close is surprisingly gentle."

Maya attached a short video clip and a selection of the day's best photos to her journal entry. She also added location data, automatically tagging the entry with GPS coordinates for future reference.

THE SCIENCE OF TRAVEL AND NATURE JOURNALING

Recent studies have highlighted the benefits of combining travel, nature exposure, and journaling:

- A 2019 study in the Journal of Environmental Psychology found that nature journaling increased participants' connection to nature and overall well-being.
- Research published in the Annals of Tourism Research in 2020 showed that travelers who kept journals during their trips reported higher levels of satisfaction and more vivid, long-lasting memories of their experiences.
- A neuroscience study from University College London demonstrated that the act of drawing, even for non-artists, enhances memory and understanding of objects and scenes.

DEVELOPING YOUR PRACTICE: LESSONS FROM THE FIELD

As Olivia, Zoe, Alex, and Maya developed their travel and nature journaling practices, they discovered several key insights:

1. **Embrace Imperfection**: Not every sketch will be a masterpiece. The goal is to capture the essence of a moment or place, not create a photorealistic rendering.
2. **Use All Your Senses**: Don't just focus on what you see. Incorporate sounds, smells, textures, and even tastes into your journal entries.
3. **Mix Media**: Combine sketches, written observations, photos, found objects, and even audio recordings to create a rich, multi-dimensional record.
4. **Make Time**: Set aside dedicated time for journaling during your travels. Even 15 minutes a day can result in a treasured record of your experiences.
5. **Be Flexible**: Sometimes conditions won't be ideal for journaling. Be prepared to adapt your practice to different environments and situations.
6. **Focus on Details**: While capturing sweeping vistas can be thrilling, don't forget to notice and record the small details that make a place unique.

7. **Practice Regularly:** Like any skill, travel and nature journaling improves with consistent practice. Make it a habit, even when you're not traveling.

As the stars began to emerge above the Serengeti, Maya added a final note to her journal:

"Every time I put stylus to screen or pen to paper, I'm not just recording what I see. I'm deepening my connection to this moment, this place. My journal is more than a record of my travels; it's a map of my journey as an observer, an artist, and a human being in this vast and beautiful world."

She closed her tablet, took a deep breath of the cool night air, and smiled. Tomorrow would bring new wonders to discover and capture in her ever-growing journal.

As you embark on your own travel and nature journaling journey, remember the experiences of Olivia, Zoe, Alex, and Maya. Your journal is more than just a travel diary; it's a tool for deepening your connection to the world around you, honing your powers of observation, and creating a rich, personal record of your adventures.

Whether you're scaling mountain peaks, exploring bustling cities, trekking through rainforests, or simply observing nature in your own backyard, your journal is waiting to help you see the world with new eyes. What will you discover on your next page?

As we've explored the power of journaling to capture our experiences in nature and on our travels, we've seen how different tools - from watercolor pencils to voice recorders - can enhance our practice. Yet technology continues to evolve, offering new ways to understand and connect through our journaling. For some, like Rachel, this evolution arrives at a moment of critical decision, when traditional methods alone no longer yield the insights we seek...

SIXTEEN

AI-ENHANCED JOURNALING: HUMAN CONNECTION IN A DIGITAL AGE

Rachel's hand trembled as she opened another leather-bound journal, adding it to the towering stacks surrounding her office floor. Fifteen years of her life filled these pages – somewhere in here lay the answer about whether to accept the CEO position in Singapore.

The sun had set hours ago. Her phone buzzed again – her husband, Mark, was probably wondering why she wasn't home for dinner. The decision deadline loomed tomorrow, and manually reviewing years of entries had yielded little clarity beyond mounting frustration and paper cuts.

"There has to be a better way," she muttered, reaching for her phone. Her finger hovered over an app her colleague Michael had mentioned during lunch. He'd described it as "like having a brilliant reader who never forgets a word you've written."

The idea of sharing her private thoughts with AI made her stomach clench. But as she glanced at the scattered journals, desperation won over doubt. With trembling fingers, she downloaded Claude 3.5 Sonnet.

"Welcome," appeared on her screen. "Would you like to begin with a current reflection or analyze existing journal entries?"

Rachel took a deep breath. "I need to make a life-changing decision by tomorrow, and I know I've written about similar choices before. Can you help me find patterns in my decision-making?"

"I'd be happy to help you explore patterns in your past decisions. Would you like to share some key entries, focusing on major life choices you've made?"

Rachel picked up her most recent journal. "I should warn you – my handwriting gets messy when I'm stressed."

"I can analyze handwritten text through photos, looking for both content and emotional indicators through handwriting analysis. Shall we start with a recent entry about this decision?"

She positioned her phone camera over yesterday's tear-stained page. As she watched the AI process the image, a notification popped up from another journaling app – ChatGPT 4.0, also recommended by Michael. "Enhanced visual pattern recognition," he'd said. "Great for seeing the bigger picture."

Rachel hesitated. One AI was already pushing her comfort zone. But as she looked at the decades of scattered insights surrounding her, she realized this decision might require every tool available.

IMPORTANT NOTE ABOUT AI TECHNOLOGY

As of this book's publication, artificial intelligence is evolving at an unprecedented pace. The tools, features, and capabilities described in this chapter represent a snapshot of what was available during writing. By the time you read this, significant changes will likely have occurred in AI technology.

What Will Change:

- AI models and their capabilities
- Available journaling platforms and features
- Integration options and compatibility
- Privacy considerations and security protocols
- User interfaces and interaction methods
- Pricing structures and accessibility
- Data handling and privacy regulations

What Remains Constant:

- The fundamental purpose of journaling for self-reflection
- The importance of maintaining privacy and personal boundaries
- The value of authentic self-expression
- The need for balance between technology and traditional practices
- The core principles of meaningful journaling

For the most current information about AI journaling tools, techniques, and considerations, visit: richardfrench.net/category/journaling

THE POWER OF PATTERN RECOGNITION

Within an hour, Rachel had photographed key decision points from her journals. Claude analyzed her handwriting pressure, noting increased anxiety around career choices. Meanwhile, ChatGPT studied the visual layout of her entries – how her neat margins dissolved into chaotic scribbles during times of stress.

"I notice a pattern," Claude observed. "When faced with major changes, you often list practical considerations first, but your final decisions typically align with family impact. Would you like to explore this theme?"

Rachel sat back, stunned. She'd never noticed this pattern herself.

Her phone buzzed – Michael again. She answered this time.

"Still at the office?" he asked. "The weekly family insight session just flagged something interesting. Mind if I stop by?"

Twenty minutes later, Michael pulled up a chair beside Rachel's journal-strewn desk. He opened his tablet, showing a dashboard that made her data scientist heart skip.

"Each family member uses their preferred journaling tool," he explained. "Sarah loves Day One's clean interface. Emma's college anxiety led her to ThoughtFlow's therapy integration. Lucy's artistic – she uses Mem.ai for visual journaling.

Michael pulled up Lucy's visual journaling workspace. "Lucy's approach is unique," he explained. "Mem.ai lets her combine sketches, photos, and notes in what she calls her 'mood maps.' The AI doesn't just store these elements - it finds connections between them."

"For instance," he demonstrated, "when Lucy photographs her pottery projects, the AI analyzes not just the images but also her notes about the creative process. It might be noticed that her most innovative pieces come after she's spent time in nature or that certain color choices correlate with specific emotions. It's like having an art therapist who can read both the obvious and subtle messages in her creative expression."

Michael continued, "Once a week, our meta-analysis AI examines patterns across all journals."

He pulled up a recent report. "Look here – when I was considering that position in Boston, our collective anxiety spiked. But the AI spotted something human readers missed: each family member wrote, on their own, about missing Sunday dinners with grandma."

Rachel leaned closer. "The job would've doubled my salary," Michael continued, "but that one insight made the decision clear. Some patterns only emerge when you have the right tools to spot them."

He glanced at her scattered journals. "Want to see how the meta-analysis works with historical entries?"

FAMILY SYSTEMS AND SHARED INSIGHTS

Michael opened his tablet's security settings. "First thing – each journal remains private. The meta-analysis only sees patterns, never content. Emma was adamant about that," he smiled.

Michael demonstrated their family's privacy system. "Think of it like each person having their own private diary," he explained. "But instead of just a lock and key, we have several layers of protection. First, all family member's entries are scrambled into code that only they can unlock. Second, when the AI looks for patterns, it's like having a trusted friend who can tell you're happy or sad without knowing the specific details of why. Finally, when we share insights as a family, we only see things like 'three people felt excited today' without knowing who or why."

The family's sharing screen used colors to show different moods -- like a mood ring for the whole family. Red showed when someone was stressed, blue for peaceful times, and yellow when feelings were mixed.

"Check this out," he said, importing a sample of Rachel's recent entries. The system began reading Rachel's entries, much like a thoughtful friend might read through her old journals. "Watch how it works," Michael explained. "First, it notices the basics - like how often you mention feeling worried or excited. Then, it looks deeper, finding connections you might miss. For instance, it might notice that you tend to write longer entries when making big decisions or that your language becomes more uncertain when discussing career changes.

"The clever part," he continued, "is how it compares these patterns with others' experiences - without ever sharing the private details. It's like having a wise mentor who's helped hundreds of people through similar decisions but maintains everyone's confidentiality."

"Your sleep disruption pattern matches Sarah's from last year's career shift," he noted. "And see this emotional curve? Similar to Emma's college decision stress."

Rachel studied the visualizations. "But how do you ensure privacy when—"

A notification interrupted: Lucy had started her evening art journal session. A new node appeared on Michael's dashboard, pulsing with creative energy as his younger daughter processed her day through AI-enhanced digital painting.

"Each person maintains their sanctuary," Michael explained. "Lucy's AI analyzes brush strokes and color choices. Emma's tracks cognitive patterns. Sarah's focuses on narrative analysis. The meta-system looks for resonance between these different types of data."

Michael opened the family's combined dashboard. "Think of this as a family dinner table where everyone's journals can have a conversation," he explained. "But instead of sharing private details, it's more like understanding the melody of each person's day and how those melodies harmonize - or sometimes create discord."

"For example," he pointed to a recent pattern, "last week, everyone's entries showed increasing excitement, but in different ways. Lucy's artwork used brighter colors, Emma's writing became more ener-getic, and Sarah's voice journals had a more upbeat tone. The system noticed this shared positive trend without needing to know the private reasons behind it."

"It's particularly helpful," he added, "for noticing when one family member might need support. If someone's patterns start showing stress while everyone else is calm, we can reach out - not because we know what's wrong, but because we know they might need a little extra care."

He pulled up his own journal interface – stark, data-driven, with clear metrics and trend lines. "I prefer this view, but..." He swiped to a family insights page. "This weekly synthesis helps us support each other without invading privacy. Last month, it spotted Lucy's increasing academic anxiety through her artwork before she even mentioned it."

FROM INDIVIDUAL TO FAMILY PRACTICE

Rachel stared at the dashboard, her mind racing with possibilities. "Could we analyze my family's patterns? I haven't even asked Mark and the kids how they'd feel about Singapore."

"Let's set it up," Michael said, creating a secure family group. "Each person needs to choose their preferred journaling tool first."

That evening, Rachel sat at her kitchen table with Mark and their teenagers, Jamie and Sophie. "I need to make a big decision," she began, "and I'd like to try something new."

Sophie, sixteen and tech-savvy, immediately downloaded Thought-Flow. "My friend Emma uses this for college prep anxiety," she said. "The art therapy module is amazing."

Sophie showed Rachel how ThoughtFlow worked with her art therapy journaling. "See, Mom? When I sketch while writing about college applications, it analyzes both my words and my drawings. Yesterday, I was writing about portfolio deadlines and unconsciously drawing tight spirals - the AI noticed this pattern and suggested some breathing exercises."

"It also has this cool feature," Sophie continued, pulling up her weekly view. "It creates a visual story of my emotions. The size of my drawings, the colors I choose, even how hard I press with the pencil - it combines all of this with my written words to show me patterns. Like here, when my art started using darker colors, it asked if I wanted to explore why, helping me realize I was putting too much pressure on myself."

Jamie, thirteen and skeptical at first, perked up when Rachel mentioned privacy features. "So no one can read my actual entries? Not even you?"

"Mark selected Claude for his journaling. "It's like having a conversational partner who remembers everything we've discussed," he explained to Rachel. "When I write about my startup worries, it notices patterns I miss. For example, last week, it pointed out that my anxiety peaks before investor meetings but drops once I start presenting. It even reminded me of similar situations from past entries where pushing through the initial nervousness led to success."

"What I really appreciate," Mark added, opening his journal app, "is how it helps me dig deeper. If I write something like 'today was rough,' it might ask, 'I notice this echoes your entry from last month - what feels different about today's challenges?' It's not just recording my thoughts; it's helping me understand them better."

Over the next three days, they journaled on their own. Rachel found herself looking forward to the first family analysis, scheduled for Thursday evening. The decision deadline had been extended a week after she'd explained her new approach to the board.

When Thursday arrived, they gathered in the living room. Rachel's hands shook as she initiated the first meta-analysis.

The dashboard illuminated with unexpected insights: Jamie's entries revealed excitement about potential Asian gaming connections; Sophie's art journals showed recurring Singapore-inspired themes from her architecture research; Mark's startup plans aligned better with Asian markets.

But one pattern stood out starkly — their collective entries showed stronger family bonds during periods of shared adventure than in times of stable routine.

"Mom, look at this," Sophie pointed to a rippling line of blue across the weekly analysis. "When we moved here from Boston, your journals showed worry, but mine showed adventure. The AI says that pattern's repeating now."

Rachel studied the interwoven patterns of their family's entries. Colors shifted and merged: Mark's entrepreneurial energy in green, Jamie's gaming excitement in purple, and Sophie's architectural inspirations in orange.

"There's more," Mark added, highlighting a cluster of connected nodes. "Our strongest family moments aren't about location — they're about shared growth. Remember the disaster of camping in Maine?"

Jamie laughed. "When Dad tried to start a fire in the rain?"

"Exactly," Mark said. "The AI found similar patterns of family bonding through challenges across all our journals. Singapore isn't just your opportunity, Rachel. It's ours."

A notification popped up on Rachel's screen. Claude had completed its analysis of her historical entries, finding a clear pattern: her biggest regrets weren't from taking chances, but from letting fear prevent them.

She opened her journal app, ready to write about her decision, when she noticed another member had been added to their family group – her mother.

"I set it up," Sophie explained. "Grandma's using the voice journaling feature in Day One. The AI can analyze her stories alongside our entries. Distance doesn't matter anymore."

Rachel began to write, her fingers steady now. The AI assistant noted her changed writing rhythm and the confidence in her keystrokes. As she typed, the family dashboard pulsed with synchronized patterns of excitement and possibility.

EXPANDING HORIZONS: THE COMMUNITY IMPACT

At the next journaling circle meeting, Rachel shared her family's approach. William, still clutching his leather-bound notebook, leaned forward with unexpected interest.

"Show me those pattern visualizations again," he asked. As a novelist, he'd resisted AI assistance until now. But watching the interplay of family dynamics on Rachel's dashboard stirred his storyteller's imagination.

Madison showed her students how to use AI insights to strengthen their storytelling. "We started small," she explained. "First, students used the AI to track their characters' emotional journeys through their drafts - like having a sensitivity reader who could spot when a character's actions didn't match their personality. Then, we expanded to analyzing plot structures, where the AI would highlight patterns like pacing problems or underdeveloped themes. The students could even compare their story patterns with classic literature, seeing how their character development matched or differed from traditional story arcs.

"For example," Madison continued, pulling up a student's dashboard, "Sarah here discovered that her protagonist's emotional growth flatlined in the middle chapters. The AI showed this by comparing the character's dialogue patterns and actions across the story. Sarah used this insight to revise those chapters, adding more meaningful character development moments."

Dr. Thompson, who'd been quietly observing, opened her laptop. "I've been experimenting with something similar in group therapy." Her screen displayed a modified version of the meta-analysis system, tracking collective healing patterns while maintaining individual privacy.

"The possibilities for community connection are remarkable," she explained. "One group noticed their anxiety patterns shifted in sync with local events. Another discovered shared childhood experiences through theme analysis."

Word spread. Within months, other groups adapted the framework:

- A startup incubator tracking team dynamics
- A grief support circle monitoring healing patterns
- A high school journalism class analyzing community stories
- An environmental group correlating nature experiences

Rachel watched her family's dashboard pulse with daily insights. Jamie had started a gaming journal group, their collective entries revealing patterns in strategy and collaboration. Sophie's architecture class used visual journaling to track design evolution. Mark's startup team adopted pattern analysis for product development.

But the most surprising impact came from her mother's voice journals. Other seniors at her retirement community began sharing stories, creating an oral history project enhanced by AI pattern recognition. Geographic distance dissolved as families connected through shared narratives and insights.

Rachel and Michael sat in his home office, surrounded by holographic displays of their evolved journaling system. What had started as family insights had grown into something more sophisticated.

"Watch this new feature," Michael said, gesturing to a floating visualization. "The AI now recognizes emotional patterns across different forms of expression – Sophie's architectural sketches, Jamie's game strategies, your mother's voice patterns."

He showed Rachel how the system protected everyone's privacy: each journal had its own special digital lock, like a high-tech diary key. The system kept careful track of who could see what, similar to a trusted librarian who knows which books are private. Most importantly, while the AI could spot helpful patterns across different journals, it was like finding common themes in a book club without revealing who wrote what.

"Each group adapts it differently," Rachel noted, scrolling through anonymized examples:

The high school journalism class had uncovered a pattern of environmental concerns in student stories. Their AI system now correlates local pollution data with community narratives.

William's writing group tracked character authenticity across different authors' works, helping new writers develop more nuanced storytelling.

Dr. Thompson's therapy groups used pattern recognition to identify collective healing milestones while protecting individual privacy.

"But the core remains simple," Michael said, pulling up his family's evening dashboard. Lucy's art journal pulsed with creative energy as she worked on college portfolio pieces. The system noted correlations between her color choices and Emma's written reflections on freshman year.

Sarah's voice journal added another layer — the AI analyzing tone and word choice to track family well-being. A new pattern emerged: their strongest connections happened during these evening hours when each family member wrote in their own way while remaining digitally linked.

Rachel checked her own family's dashboard. Jamie was gaming, his strategic decisions flowing into the pattern analysis. Sophie's architectural journal showed late-night inspiration. Mark's entrepreneur's log tracked emerging ideas. Her mother's voice journal hummed with stories from her day.

CROSS-CULTURAL CONNECTIONS: THE SINGAPORE JOURNEY

Three months into life in Singapore, Rachel's family gathered for their weekly insight review. The dashboard displayed an intricate web of their cross-continental connections.

"Look at this convergence," Sophie pointed. Her architectural studies at Singapore Polytechnic flowed into the pattern analysis, revealing unexpected parallels with Jamie's gaming strategies in multiplayer Asian servers.

Mark's startup journal throbbed with excitement. "The AI spotted something fascinating," he said. "My business insights peak during our morning calls with Mom — her stories about small-town life somehow trigger innovation patterns."

The system highlighted a new trend: their family bonds had strengthened across the distance. Daily journals, analyzed collectively, showed deeper appreciation for their shared adventure. Jamie's gaming journals revealed growing confidence in cross-cultural friendships. Sophie's architectural drawings incorporated elements of both Eastern and Western design, reflecting their family's evolving identity.

Rachel opened her CEO journal, its patterns interweaving with her personal entries. The AI noted how her leadership style had evolved, influenced by her family's collective adaptation to change.

A notification chimed – Dr. Thompson's global journaling study wanted to include their family's anonymized patterns. Their story of digital connection across cultures was proving valuable to other families navigating international moves.

"Dad, check this out," Jamie said, highlighting a pattern cluster. His gaming journal had captured the moment their family dynamic shifted – from fear of separation to excitement about their expanded world.

Rachel studied the interwoven digital threads connecting their lives across continents. What had begun as a decision-making tool had become their family's strength, growing stronger with each shared insight.

The AI flagged a unique pattern in Rachel's family journals: cultural adaptation wasn't linear but cyclic. Each family member experienced it differently:

Sophie's Architectural Journal:

"Today I understood why Singapore's void decks matter. They're not just empty spaces – they're community hearts. Incorporating this concept into my designs changed everything. The AI noted how my sketches evolved from purely functional to community-centered."

The AI prompt responded: "Your drawings show increasing integration of communal spaces. Would you like to explore how this reflects your own journey of finding community here?"

Jamie's Gaming Log:

"Raiding with my Singapore team is different. It's not just about strategy – it's about harmony. The AI helped me see how my

gaming style adapted, becoming more collaborative than competitive."

Pattern Analysis: *Gaming interactions show a 60% increase in team-based decisions and, a 45% decrease in solo plays.*

Mark's Startup Chronicles:

"Failed pitch today. AI analysis showed I was using Western business patterns. Adjusted approach after reviewing local partnership customs. Second attempt succeeded."

AI Insight: *"Notice how your communication patterns shift between markets. Your most successful negotiations blend approaches."*

Rachel's mother added unexpected depth through her voice journals:

"In my day, letters took weeks to cross oceans. Now I watch my grandchildren grow daily. The distance feels different."

The system correlated her stories with family patterns, revealing how traditional wisdom adapted to modern challenges.

Dr. Thompson incorporated these insights into her global family therapy framework. "Each family creates their own digital culture," she explained. "The AI helps them recognize and strengthen their unique patterns."

FUTURE IMPLICATIONS

The sun set over Singapore's skyline as Rachel reviewed their two-year journey. Her family's dashboard displayed evolving patterns:

- Sophie's architectural designs now seamlessly blended cultures
- Jamie moderated global gaming communities
- Mark's startup operated across continents
- Her mother's stories reached a worldwide audience

The AI highlighted a profound shift: their journals had become more than personal records. They were nodes in a growing network of human experience, each entry contributing to a deeper understanding of family, culture, and connection.

William's novel, informed by these patterns, reached international audiences. Madison's students collaborated with peers worldwide. Dr. Thompson's therapy groups found strength in shared experiences across cultures.

"The future of journaling," Rachel wrote in her evening entry, "isn't about better technology. It's about a deeper understanding of human connection."

The AI noted her words, adding them to the pattern analysis that now helped families worldwide navigate change while staying connected.

Transforming the Journaling Community

The journaling circle met in its usual coffee shop, but the conversation had evolved far beyond their early discussions of AI integration. William, once the strongest advocate for purely traditional journaling, now led a worldwide network of novelists using pattern analysis to develop authentic characters.

"Last week," he shared, opening his leather journal alongside his tablet, "our writing group connected with authors in Tokyo and Mumbai. The AI found universal emotional patterns in how we describe family relationships, despite our cultural differences."

Madison nodded, pulling up her classroom dashboard. "My students collaborate with writing groups in five countries now. The AI helps them recognize shared themes in their coming-of-age stories while respecting the unique cultural context of each narrative."

Dr. Thompson's therapy practice has expanded globally. "We're seeing something remarkable," she explained. "When families in transition see the pattern analysis from others who've made similar journeys, it normalizes their experience. A family moving from Seoul to Sydney can learn from the adaptation patterns of a family that moved from London to Bangkok."

The impact rippled through various communities:

Education

- Writing classes connected across continents
- Students sharing cultural perspectives through guided journals
- Teachers tracking collective learning patterns
- Cross-cultural writing projects flourishing

Mental Health

Local support groups discovered their experiences echoed worldwide:

- Grief patterns showing universal stages across cultures
- Anxiety manifests in varied ways but healing similarly
- Recovery journeys strengthened by global connections
- Therapeutic insights enriched by diverse perspectives

Creative Communities

Artists and writers found new depths:

- Story patterns revealing universal human experiences
- Character development enriched by global insights
- Creative blocks solved through pattern recognition
- Collaborative projects spanning continents

Family Systems

The Anderson family's approach inspired new frameworks:

- Multi-generational story preservation
- Cross-cultural family bonding
- Distance-bridging communication patterns
- Shared growth tracking

Business Applications

Companies adopted modified versions:

- Team dynamics analysis
- Cross-cultural collaboration insights
- Innovation pattern tracking
- Global project management

Rachel observed these changes from her Singapore office, where she now mentored other families navigating international transitions. "The technology matters less than the connections it enables," she noted in her journal. "We're not just sharing stories anymore – we're weaving a global tapestry of human experience."

The AI flagged her words, linking them to similar insights from journal entries worldwide. In retirement communities, college dorms, corporate offices, and family homes across the globe, people were discovering that their most personal thoughts, when analyzed for patterns, while maintaining privacy, contributed to a deeper understanding of the human connection.

"The future of journaling," Dr. Thompson reflected, "has become less about individual reflection and more about conscious participation in the human story. Each journal entry, while remaining private, adds to our collective understanding of how to navigate life's challenges and celebrate its joys."

William closed his notebook with a familiar thump, but now the sound carried a different meaning. "We haven't lost the intimacy of personal journaling," he said. "We've expanded it to embrace our shared humanity."

The circle's quiet murmur of agreement was echoed in journaling communities worldwide, each adding their unique voice to the evolving conversation about what it means to be human in an interconnected world.

THE BRIDGE BETWEEN PERSONAL AND UNIVERSAL: A CONCLUSION

As the sun set over Singapore, Rachel opened her journal for her evening reflection. Two years had passed since that night in her Boston office, surrounded by scattered journals and facing a life-changing decision. Now, her family's journaling practice had become both an anchor and compass, helping them navigate their new life while staying connected to their roots.

But their story was just one thread in a larger tapestry.

"The true power," she wrote, "isn't in the technology. It's in how it helps us see ourselves in others' stories."

From Individual to Universal: The New Journaling Landscape

Dr. Thompson's research revealed what many had discovered organically: AI-enhanced journaling wasn't replacing traditional practice but expanding it. Personal insights analyzed, while maintaining privacy, contributed to collective understanding while remaining deeply private.

William, reading from his latest novel at the journaling circle, smiled as he shared how pattern analysis had helped him create more authentic characters. "Our stories," he said, "are both unique and universal. The AI just helps us see the connections."

IMPORTANT NOTE ABOUT AI TECHNOLOGY

As of this book's publication, artificial intelligence is evolving at an unprecedented pace. The tools, features, and capabilities described in this chapter represent a snapshot of what was available during writing. By the time you read this, significant changes will likely have occurred in AI technology.

What Will Change:

- AI models and their capabilities
- Available journaling platforms and features
- Integration options and compatibility
- Privacy considerations and security protocols
- User interfaces and interaction methods
- Pricing structures and accessibility
- Data handling and privacy regulations

What Remains Constant:

- The fundamental purpose of journaling for self-reflection
- The importance of maintaining privacy and personal boundaries
- The value of authentic self-expression
- The need for a balance between technology and traditional practices
- The core principles of meaningful journaling

For the most current information about AI journaling tools, techniques, and considerations, visit: richardfrench.net/category/journaling

This dedicated resource is regularly updated with:

- Reviews of new AI journaling tools

- Security and privacy guidelines
- Best practices for AI integration
- User experiences and case studies
- Emerging trends and technologies
- Tips for maintaining authenticity
- Troubleshooting guides

Remember: The technology that supports your journaling practice will continue to evolve, but your authentic voice and personal insights remain the heart of the experience. Choose tools that enhance rather than overshadow your natural reflection process, and always prioritize the privacy and integrity of your personal narrative.

PRACTICAL GUIDE TO AI-ENHANCED JOURNALING

For those beginning this journey, here are the essential steps:

1. **Choose Your Entry Point**

- Start with one trusted platform
- Focus on personal comfort level
- Begin with basic features
- Expand at a comfortable pace

2. **Establish Your Foundation**

Privacy First:

- Enable encryption
- Set clear boundaries
- Regular security reviews
- Data backup protocol

Basic Practice:

- Morning reflection (5-10 minutes)
- Evening review (10-15 minutes)
- Weekly pattern analysis
- Monthly insight review

3. Select Your Tools

Based on your primary needs:

- Emotional insight: Claude 3.5 Sonnet
- Visual analysis: ChatGPT 4.0
- Traditional feel: Day One + AI
- Therapeutic focus: ThoughtFlow
- Family connection: Meta-analysis systems

4. Build Your Practice

Start with simple prompts:

- "What patterns do I notice today?"
- "How does this connect to past experiences?"
- "What insights emerge from today's entries?"
- "What feelings arise as I write?"

5. Consider Family Integration

If expanding to family practice:

- Individual choice of tools
- Clear privacy protocols
- Weekly family reviews
- Pattern-only sharing
- Meta-analysis insights

6. Join the Larger Conversation

- Connect with journaling groups
- Share anonymized insights
- Participate in research
- Contribute to collective understanding

REMEMBER

As Madison often reminds her students: "Your journal remains your sanctuary. The AI is just a thoughtful companion on your journey of self-discovery."

The future of journaling extends beyond the personal to the universal, while protecting the sacred space of individual reflection. Each entry, whether handwritten in a leather-bound journal or typed into an AI-enhanced app, adds to our understanding of the human experience.

Rachel closed her journal, watching Singapore's lights twinkle below. On her dashboard, she could see her family's evening journaling activity: Sophie's architectural insights flowing into her designs, Jamie's gaming strategies evolving with his international team,

Mark's business inspiration sparked by morning calls with Grandma.

Their journals had become more than records of their lives. They were bridges - between past and future, between cultures and generations, between the deeply personal and the shared human experience.

Your journal can be such a bridge too. Whether you choose to incorporate AI assistance or maintain a purely traditional practice, remember that your story, while being your own, echoes in the larger human narrative.

Begin where you are. Write what's true for you. The connections will emerge on their own, one entry at a time.

As Rachel's family continued their journey, their AI-enhanced practice became part of a longer story - one that would unfold over years and continents. Their experience highlights a crucial truth about journaling: whether enhanced by technology or purely traditional, the true value emerges through consistent practice over time...

SEVENTEEN
DREAM JOURNALING

Liam's eyes snapped open, heart racing. The vivid images from his dream still danced behind his eyelids, already starting to fade like mist in the morning sunlight. He fumbled for the notebook and pen he'd placed on his nightstand the night before, determined not to let this one slip away like so many dreams before.

CAPTURING THE EPHEMERAL: LIAM'S FIRST STEPS

With shaky handwriting, Liam began to scribble:

"I was in a house, but not my house. Old, creaky. The smell of dust and something sweet... cookies? Looking for something important. Can't remember what. Rooms kept changing. Opened a door and suddenly I was underwater, but I could breathe. Fish swam by, glowing like neon signs. There was music, familiar but couldn't place it. Felt urgent, like I needed to find something before time ran out..."

As he wrote, more details surfaced. Liam added them haphazardly, not worrying about order or coherence:

"Blue wallpaper with silver stars. Grandfather clock but hands spinning backward. Photo frames on walls but all the faces were blurred. A feeling of being watched. Not scared, but unsettled. Key in my pocket, heavy and warm."

When the flow of memories slowed, Liam sat back, surprised by how much he'd remembered. The dream was still bizarre and fragmented, but having it on paper made it feel more real and less likely to evaporate completely.

TECHNIQUES FOR RECALL: SOFIA'S DREAM LAB

Across town, Sofia was turning dream journaling into an art form. A psychology student fascinated by the subconscious mind, she'd been honing her recall techniques for months. Her bedside table looked like a small laboratory: notebook, pen with a soft light attached, voice recorder, and even a small aromatherapy diffuser.

As she stirred from a vivid dream, Sofia remained still, eyes closed, using a technique she'd practiced:

- She took three deep breaths, anchoring herself in the liminal space between sleep and wakefulness.
- Starting with her toes and moving upward, she did a quick body scan, noting any physical sensations linked to the dream.
- She recalled the last image from her dream, then worked backward, like rewinding a movie.

Only then did Sofia reach for her voice recorder, whispering:

"Dream fragment: Standing on a stage. Spotlight so bright it hurts. The audience is there but I can't see them. Try to speak but no sound comes out. Look down, I'm wearing a suit of armor. Heavy, can barely move. The

feeling of expectation, like everyone's waiting for me to do something important. Sense of failure, inadequacy. The armor starts to rust, falling apart. As it crumbles away, I feel lighter, stronger. Finally, find my voice, but can't remember what I said. Woke up with a feeling of relief and empowerment."

Later, Sofia would transcribe this recording, adding sketches and noting any emotions or physical sensations she remembered. She'd developed a color-coding system: red for intense emotions, blue for recurring symbols, and green for potential real-life connections.

ANALYZING PATTERNS: JARED'S DREAM DATABASE

Jared stared at his computer screen, scrolling through months of dream journal entries. As a data analyst by day, he couldn't help but bring that mindset to his dream journaling practice. He'd created a spreadsheet to track recurring themes, symbols, and emotions across his dreams.

His latest entry read:

"Dream 127: Flying over a city made of books. Buildings were giant stacks of texts, streets were rivers of words. Felt exhilarated but also overwhelmed, like there was too much to read, too much to know. Spotted a golden book at the top of the tallest tower, and tried to reach it but kept getting blown off course by strong winds. Woke up feeling frustrated but also curious."

Jared added tags to his entry: #flying, #books, #overwhelm, #quest

He then updated his dream statistics:

- Flying dreams: 24% of all recorded dreams
- Dreams involving books or reading: 37%
- Dreams with feelings of overwhelm: 52%
- Dreams featuring a quest or search: 43%

Patterns began to emerge. Jared noticed that his flying dreams often coincided with periods of high stress at work, while dreams about books tended to occur when he was grappling with a big decision.

LUCID DREAMING: MAYA'S CONSCIOUS EXPLORATIONS

Maya settled into bed, excited for the night ahead. After months of practice, she'd begun to achieve lucid dreams – dreams where she was aware she was dreaming and could exert some control over the dreamscape.

She had a routine:

1. Reality checks throughout the day (like trying to push her finger through her palm) to build the habit of questioning her reality.
2. Meditation before bed to calm her mind.
3. Setting a clear intention: "I will become aware that I'm dreaming."
4. Visualizing her desired dream scenario as she fell asleep.

That night, Maya found herself walking through a forest. The leaves were an impossible shade of purple, which triggered her lucidity. "I'm dreaming," she realized. Instead of waking up, she stayed calm and decided to explore.

She flew between the trees, marveling at the detail her mind could create. She summoned dream characters and engaged them in conversation, asking, "What message does my subconscious have for me?" The answers were often surprising and insightful.

Upon waking, Maya immediately reached for her dream journal:

"Lucid dream achieved! Forest setting, flying, remarkable clarity. Asked about my career dilemma. The dream character (looked like my old profes-

sor) said, 'The path you fear is the one you need.' Felt a strong sense of truth. Also: everything smelled like cinnamon. Note: Research symbolism of cinnamon."

THE SCIENCE OF DREAM JOURNALING

Recent studies have shed light on the benefits of dream journaling:

- A 2018 study in the journal Consciousness and Cognition found that people who regularly record their dreams show increased dream recall and report more creative problem-solving abilities in waking life.
- Research published in Frontiers in Psychology in 2019 demonstrated that dream content often reflects waking-life concerns and experiences, suggesting that analyzing dreams can provide insights into one's psychological state.
- A 2020 study in the Journal of Sleep Research showed that lucid dreaming practices, including dream journaling, can lead to improvements in metacognitive ability and self-reflection skills.

INTEGRATING DREAM INSIGHTS: FROM SUBCONSCIOUS TO CONSCIOUS

As Liam, Sofia, Jared, and Maya developed their dream journaling practices, they discovered ways to integrate dream insights into their waking lives:

1. **Emotional Processing**: Sofia noticed that recording and reflecting on her dreams helped her process complex emotions she was struggling with in her waking life.
2. **Creative Inspiration**: Liam, an aspiring writer, found that his vivid dream descriptions were improving his creative

writing skills. He even turned one recurring dream into a short story.

3. **Problem Solving**: Jared realized that his dreams often presented metaphorical solutions to work problems. He started incubating specific questions before sleep, often waking with fresh perspectives.

4. **Personal Growth**: Maya used her lucid dreams as a tool for self-exploration and growth, confronting fears and practicing new behaviors in the safe space of her dreams.

5. **Improved Sleep Quality**: All four found that the practice of dream journaling made them more attuned to their sleep patterns, leading to better sleep hygiene and quality.

As the months passed, their dream journals became more than just records of nightly adventures. They were roadmaps of the subconscious, offering glimpses into hidden fears, desires, and untapped potential.

Liam, flipping through his journal one evening, wrote a reflection:

"Six months ago, I thought dreams were just random firings of a sleeping brain. Now I see them as nightly expeditions into the depths of my psyche. My dream journal has become a conversation with parts of myself I never knew existed. I've discovered creativity I didn't know I possessed, confronted fears I didn't realize were holding me back, and found wisdom in the most unexpected places. The boundary between sleeping and waking feels more permeable now, in the best possible way. I'm more aware, and more alive in both states. What started as a curiosity has become an invaluable tool for self-discovery and growth."

As you embark on your own dream journaling journey, remember the experiences of Liam, Sofia, Jared, and Maya. Your dream journal is more than a collection of nightly stories; it's a bridge between your conscious and subconscious mind, a tool for deepening your self-understanding and unlocking your hidden potential.

Whether you're deciphering symbolic messages, practicing lucid dreaming, analyzing patterns, or simply marveling at the creativity of your sleeping mind, your dream journal is waiting to reveal new dimensions of your inner world. What mysteries will you uncover in your dreams tonight?

EIGHTEEN
JOURNALING FOR PROFESSIONAL DEVELOPMENT

Rachel stared at her computer screen, the harsh fluorescent lights of her cubicle reflecting off the surface. Another day, another dead end. Five years into her marketing career, she felt stuck, unsure of her next move. With a sigh, she pulled out a sleek, leather-bound notebook – a gift from her mentor. "Try journaling," he'd said. "It might surprise you." Skeptical but desperate, Rachel uncapped her pen and began to write.

CAREER REFLECTION: UNCOVERING PATTERNS AND PASSIONS

"Why am I so unsatisfied? The money's good, my coworkers are nice enough, but something's missing. I dread Mondays. Is this all there is?"

As Rachel's pen moved across the page, her thoughts began to flow. She found herself recalling moments from her career:

"The product launch last year – I was stressed, but excited. Loved the creative aspects, but hated the endless meetings. That charity event we organized – long hours, but so fulfilling. Mentoring the new intern – unexpected joy in teaching others."

Without realizing it, Rachel had stumbled upon a powerful career reflection technique. By documenting specific experiences, she was uncovering patterns in what energized her and what drained her.

GOAL SETTING: FROM VAGUE DESIRES TO ACTIONABLE PLANS

Inspired by her reflections, Rachel decided to set some professional goals. But instead of vague aspirations, she remembered a framework her mentor had taught her: SMART goals.

She wrote:

*"**Current Goal**: 'Advance my career'*
SMART Version:
***Specific**: Secure a position as Marketing Team Lead*
Measurable: Apply for at least 3 internal positions, develop 2 new high-level skills
***Achievable**: I have the base experience; need to build leadership skills*
***Relevant**: Aligns with my desire for more creative control and mentoring opportunities*
***Time-bound**: Achieve within 18 months"*

Beneath this, Rachel brainstormed action steps:

1. Enroll in a leadership course (research options this week)
2. Ask for more responsibility on upcoming product launch
3. Schedule coffee with current Team Lead to understand the role better
4. Update LinkedIn profile and resume (set aside 2 hours this weekend)

The vague anxiety about her career was transforming into a concrete plan of action.

SKILLS INVENTORY: RECOGNIZING HIDDEN STRENGTHS

Carlos, a software engineer, sat in his home office, surrounded by screens displaying lines of code. He'd been passed over for a promotion again, and the rejection stung. Determined to understand why, he opened his journal and began a skills inventory.

He divided the page into three columns:

Technical Skills	Soft Skills	Skills to Develop
Java, Python, C++	Problem-solving	Public speaking
Database management	Attention to detail	Project management
API development	???	Leadership

"Wait. What are my soft skills really? I'm not sure I know."

This realization led Carlos to a deeper exploration. He began documenting specific instances where he'd used non-technical skills:

"Last week: Explained complex database issue to non-technical project manager. She said my explanation was clear and helpful. Is that a communication skill?

A month ago: Noticed inconsistency in new team member's code during review. Approached them privately, and walked through the issue together. They thanked me for not embarrassing them in the group meeting. Mentoring skill?

Ongoing: Always deliver projects on time. Coworkers often ask me to review their time estimates. Time management skill?"

As he wrote, Carlos began to see himself in a new light. He had more to offer than just technical expertise. This newfound self-awareness boosted his confidence and gave him clear areas for further development.

FEEDBACK INTEGRATION: TURNING CRITICISM INTO GROWTH

Anita, a graphic designer, cringed as she opened her journal. The client presentation hadn't gone well, and her boss's feedback was still ringing in her ears. "Your designs lack originality," he'd said. "And you need to speak up more in meetings."

Instead of letting the criticism fester, Anita decided to use her journal to process and plan:

"Initial reaction: Defensive. Hurt. Want to argue.

Deeper reflection: Is there truth here? The last few projects have felt safe, not exciting. I have been quiet in meetings lately. Fear of judgment?

Action steps:

1. Originality:

- *Spend 30 minutes daily on creative exercises unrelated to work*
- *Attend local art exhibit this weekend for inspiration*
- *Ask to shadow Senior Designer on next big project*

2. Speaking up:

- *Prepare at least one question or comment before each meeting*
- *Practice voicing opinions with trusted colleague*
- *Look into Toastmasters or other public speaking groups"*

By journaling through the feedback, Anita transformed a negative experience into a growth opportunity.

PROJECT DEBRIEFS: LEARNING FROM SUCCESSES AND FAILURES

Marcus, a project manager, had just wrapped up a major software launch. As the team celebrated, he slipped away to his office and opened his project journal. He'd made it a habit to debrief every project, win or lose.

"Project: Aurora Software Launch

Duration: 8 months

Outcome: Launched on time, within budget. Client is mostly satisfied.

What went well:

- *Agile methodology kept us flexible*
- *Daily stand-ups improved communication*
- *New QA process caught critical bugs early*

What could be improved:

- *Underestimated time for client feedback, caused a last-minute rush*
- *Team burnout in final month*
- *Documentation fell behind, need better system*

Lessons learned:

1. *Build more buffer time for client interactions*
2. *Implement better work-life balance policies for intense projects*
3. *Assign dedicated team member for documentation upkeep*

Ideas for the next project:

- *Try new project management software for better tracking*
- *Implement mid-project team satisfaction survey*
- *Schedule regular code refactoring sessions to prevent technical debt"*

This structured reflection allowed Marcus to improve his project management skills, learning from both successes and setbacks.

NETWORKING JOURNAL: BUILDING MEANINGFUL PROFESSIONAL RELATIONSHIPS

Yuki, a recent MBA graduate, felt overwhelmed at the industry conference. Hundreds of potential contacts, but how to keep track? She ducked into a quiet corner and pulled out her networking journal.

For each meaningful interaction, she noted:

*"Name: Dr. Sarah Smith
Position: Head of R&D, Innovatech
Context: Chatted after AI ethics panel
Topics Discussed: Potential of AI in healthcare, need for diverse datasets
Follow-up: Send article on AI bias in medical diagnoses
Personal Details: Passionate about rock climbing, mentioned upcoming trip to Yosemite*

*Name: Alex Rossi
Position: Senior Marketing Manager, GreenGrowth Startups
Context: Shared taxi to hotel
Topics Discussed: Challenges of marketing sustainable products, his company's expansion plans
Follow-up: Connect on LinkedIn, mention an interest in sustainability marketing
Personal Details: Originally from Italy, recommended a great pasta place in the city"*

Later, Yuki would use these notes to send personalized follow-up messages, nurturing these initial connections into valuable professional relationships.

THE SCIENCE BEHIND PROFESSIONAL DEVELOPMENT JOURNALING

Recent studies have highlighted the benefits of journaling for career growth:

- A 2019 study in the Journal of Applied Psychology found that employees who engaged in regular written reflection about their work experiences showed improved job performance and higher rates of promotion over 12 months.
- Research published in Career Development International in 2020 demonstrated that goal-setting journaling techniques increased participants' career self-efficacy and led to more proactive career behaviors.
- A 2021 study in the Journal of Occupational and Organizational Psychology showed that employees who used journaling to process workplace feedback were more likely to implement changes and show improvement in targeted areas.

INTEGRATING JOURNALING INTO PROFESSIONAL LIFE

As Rachel, Carlos, Anita, Marcus, and Yuki continued their journaling practices, they discovered key insights:

1. **Consistency is Key**: Short, regular entries were more valuable than occasional long sessions.
2. **Review and Reflect**: Periodically reviewing old entries revealed patterns and progress that weren't obvious in the day-to-day.
3. **Action-Oriented**: The most valuable journaling led to concrete actions and changes in behavior.
4. **Flexibility**: Each person adapted their journaling style to fit their personality and career needs.

5. **Honesty**: The more candid they were in their journals, the more insight they gained.
6. **Integration**: Combining journaling with other professional development activities (courses, mentoring, networking) amplified the benefits of each.

Six months into her journaling journey, Rachel wrote a reflection:

"Looking back at my first entries, I no longer recognize that frustrated, directionless person. Journaling hasn't solved all my career challenges, but it's given me clarity, direction, and a sense of agency I never had before. I'm more aware of my strengths, more intentional about my growth, and more confident in my decisions. This journal has become my career compass, my professional confidant, and my accountability partner. Whatever challenges lie ahead in my career, I know I have the tools to face them head-on."

As you embark on your own professional development journaling journey, remember the experiences of Rachel, Carlos, Anita, Marcus, and Yuki. Your journal is more than just a record of your work life; it's a powerful tool for self-discovery, goal-setting, skill development, and career navigation.

Whether you're climbing the corporate ladder, switching fields, starting a business, or simply trying to find more fulfillment in your current role, your journal is waiting to help you chart your course. What new professional heights will you reach, one page at a time?

NINETEEN

LONG-TERM JOURNALING

Eleanor's fingers traced the weathered spine of her oldest journal, a faded blue notebook she'd started on her 16th birthday. Now, on the eve of her 60th, she pulled it from the shelf along with dozens of others - a colorful chronicle of nearly half a century.

She opened the blue notebook, smiling at her loopy teenage handwriting:

"April 15, 1980

Got this journal for my birthday. Not sure what to write, but Mom says it'll be fun to look back on someday. I doubt it. Nothing exciting ever happens to me..."

Little did young Eleanor know the journey that lay ahead, or how those pages would become a map of her life's winding path.

CREATING A LIFE ARCHIVE: THE POWER OF CONSISTENCY

As Eleanor flipped through the years, she marveled at the transformation. Those first tentative entries had evolved into a rich tapestry of experiences, reflections, and growth:

"September 3, 1985
First day of college. Terrified and exhilarated. Roommate seems nice, but I miss home already. Can I really do this?"

"July 12, 1992
Mark proposed! By the lake, at sunset. I'm over the moon but also scared. Are we ready for this step?"

"February 18, 2000
Held Emma for the first time today. I've never known love like this. How can someone so tiny turn your whole world upside down?"

"November 4, 2010
Dad's gone. The funeral was beautiful, but I feel hollow. How do you say goodbye to your hero?"

"March 22, 2020
Lockdown Day 10. The world's gone mad. Trying to stay positive, but it's hard. At least we have technology to stay connected."

Each entry was a snapshot, a moment frozen in time. Together, they formed a mosaic of Eleanor's life, capturing not just events, but the emotions, thoughts, and personal growth that accompanied them.

REVISITING OLD JOURNALS: A DIALOGUE WITH YOUR PAST SELF

Thomas, a 45-year-old teacher, sat at his desk, a stack of old journals beside him. He'd been feeling stuck, questioning his career choice. On a whim, he'd dug out his journals from his twenties, hoping for... what? Inspiration? Reassurance?

He opened one from his first year of teaching:

"October 15, 2003
Tough day. Jake acted out again, I lost my temper. I'm not cut out for this.
Maybe Dad was right, should've gone into accounting..."

Thomas winced, remembering that day. But as he read on, he found an entry from a few months later:

"January 22, 2004
Breakthrough with Jake today. Turns out, he's struggling at home. We talked after class, really connected. For the first time, I felt like I made a difference. This is why I wanted to teach."

As he continued reading, Thomas noticed a pattern. The challenges he faced as a new teacher weren't so different from the ones he grappled with now. But he'd overcome them before, growing and adapting along the way. His younger self's passion and resilience shone through the pages, reigniting a spark he'd thought long extinguished.

Thomas pulled out his current journal and began to write, engaging in a dialogue with his past self:

"To my younger self: Thank you for not giving up. Your struggles laid the foundation for the teacher I am today. To my future self: Remember why you started this journey. The impact you have may not always be visible, but it's real and lasting."

TRACKING PERSONAL GROWTH: MEASURING PROGRESS OVER TIME

Sophia, a 38-year-old entrepreneur, had maintained a consistent journaling practice for over a decade. As she prepared for an important investor meeting, she felt a familiar wave of self-doubt. Seeking perspective, she turned to her journals.

She created a timeline, noting key moments in her business journey:

"2012: First business idea. Excited but clueless.
2014: First failure. Devastated, but learned crucial lessons about market research.
2016: Founded current company. Ramen noodles and late nights, but so passionate.
2018: First major client. Finally feeling like a 'real' entrepreneur.
2020: Navigated pandemic pivot. Toughest challenge yet, but we survived.
2022: Expanded to international markets. Still pinching myself."

As Sophia reviewed her journey, she realized how far she'd come. The challenges that once seemed insurmountable were now valuable experiences she drew upon daily. Her journals had become a testament to her growth, resilience, and success.

Feeling reenergized, Sophia opened to a fresh page and began preparing for her investor pitch, confidence restored.

IDENTIFYING RECURRING THEMES: UNRAVELING LIFE'S PATTERNS

Dr. James Smith, a psychologist, had always encouraged his patients to journal. But it wasn't until he began analyzing his own 20 years of journals that he understood their power.

James created a color-coding system, highlighting recurring themes:

- Blue for career milestones
- Green for relationships
- Yellow for personal growth
- Red for challenges
- Purple for dreams and aspirations

As he worked through the journals, patterns emerged:

"Interesting. Every major career advance is preceded by a period of intense self-doubt and learning. It's like the uncertainty pushes me to grow."

"My relationships seem to hit rough patches every 3-4 years. But each time, the conflict leads to deeper understanding and intimacy. Is this a natural cycle?"

"I've written about wanting to write a book for over a decade. Why haven't I started? Fear of failure? Lack of time? Need to explore this further."

This analysis didn't just satisfy James's professional curiosity. It provided invaluable insights into his own behaviors, motivations, and areas for growth. Inspired, he began implementing this technique with his patients, helping them uncover their own life patterns.

THE EVOLUTION OF JOURNALING PRACTICES

As Elena approached her 70th birthday, she marveled at how her journaling practice had evolved over five decades:

1970s: Dear Diary entries about crushes and school drama

1980s: Angsty poetry and philosophical musings of a college student

1990s: Career reflections and early marriage joys/challenges

2000s: Parenting ups and downs, rediscovering personal identity

2010s: Midlife reflections, health journaling, bucket list dreams

2020s: Gratitude practices, legacy planning, pandemic reflections

Her journals had adapted to each life stage, providing exactly what she needed: a confidant, a therapist, a creativity outlet, a decision-making tool, a health tracker, and now, a legacy to pass on.

Elena opened her latest journal, a beautiful hand-bound book gifted by her granddaughter, and began to write:

"As I approach 70, I'm filled with gratitude for this lifelong journaling journey. These books are more than paper and ink; they're the story of my life, written in real time. They've witnessed my triumphs and failures, my loves and losses, my growth and setbacks. They've been a constant companion, a tool for self-discovery, and now, a bridge to the next generation.

To anyone starting this journey: stick with it. Be honest, be consistent, and be open to where it leads you. Your journals will become a priceless record of your life, a tool for growth, and a gift to your future self. The blank page is not just a record of your life; it's a space where life itself unfolds."

THE SCIENCE OF LONG-TERM JOURNALING

Recent studies have highlighted the benefits of long-term journaling:

- A 2018 longitudinal study published in the Journal of Personality and Social Psychology found that individuals who maintained consistent journaling practices over 10+ years showed higher levels of self-awareness, emotional regulation, and life satisfaction compared to non-journalers.
- Research from the University of Toronto in 2020 demonstrated that reviewing and analyzing long-term journals can lead to improved decision-making skills and a stronger sense of personal identity.
- A 2021 study in the journal Aging & Mental Health showed that older adults who engaged in life review through journaling reported reduced symptoms of depression and increased feelings of life satisfaction and meaning.

NURTURING A LIFELONG JOURNALING PRACTICE

As Eleanor, Thomas, Sophia, James, and Elena discovered, long-term journaling is more than a habit; it's a lifelong companion on your personal growth journey. Here are key insights for nurturing your practice:

1. **Embrace Evolution**: Let your journaling style and focus change as you do. What you need from journaling at 20 may be very different from what you need at 50.
2. **Consistency Over Perfection**: It's okay to have gaps or short entries. The power is in returning to the practice again and again over the years.
3. **Safe Storage**: Consider how you'll preserve your journals long-term. Digital backups, archival-quality papers, or even transcribing old journals can help ensure your life's story endures.
4. **Regular Review**: Set aside time on a regular basis to review old journals. You'll gain new insights and appreciation for your journey.
5. **Honesty is Key**: The more truthful you are in your journals, the more valuable they'll be for reflection and growth later on.
6. **Consider Your Legacy**: How might your journals impact future generations? Consider what you'd want to pass on and what should remain private.

As you continue your own journaling journey, remember the experiences of these long-term journalers. Your journal is more than a daily record; it's the story of your life as it unfolds, a tool for deep self-understanding, and a legacy of your personal growth.

Whether you're just starting out or have been journaling for decades, each entry is a step on a lifelong journey of self-discovery. What new chapters will you write in your life's story?

TWENTY
JOURNALING AND RELATIONSHIPS

Sarah stared at the blank page before her, pen hovering uncertainly. The argument with her partner, Tom, still echoed in her mind. With a deep breath, she began to write:

"I don't even know why we're fighting anymore. It started with the dishes, but it feels bigger than that. I'm so frustrated, but I don't want to say something I'll regret. Maybe if I write it out, I can figure out what's really going on..."

Little did Sarah know, this moment would be the beginning of a transformative journey, not just for her, but for her relationship as well.

INDIVIDUAL JOURNALING FOR RELATIONSHIP INSIGHT

As Sarah continued writing, her pen flew across the page:

"It's not about the dishes. It's about feeling unappreciated. I work from home, manage the household, and still feel like I'm not doing enough. But Tom doesn't see that. Or does he? Have I even told him how I feel?"

The act of journaling allowed Sarah to dig beneath the surface of her anger, uncovering the real issues at play. She realized she had been bottling up her feelings for weeks, maybe months.

On the other side of town, Tom sat in his car, a small notebook open on the steering wheel:

"I messed up. I know the dishes aren't a big deal, but Sarah seemed so upset. Am I missing something? Work has been so stressful lately, maybe I've been distant. I need to do better, but I'm not sure how."

Through their individual journaling practices, both Sarah and Tom gained clarity on their feelings and the underlying issues in their relationship.

COUPLES JOURNALING: A SHARED JOURNEY

Inspired by a relationship workshop, Sarah and Tom decided to try couples journaling. They bought a shared journal and set some ground rules:

1. Write entries at least once a week
2. Be honest, but kind
3. Focus on feelings and needs, not accusations
4. Read each other's entries with an open mind

Their first entries were tentative:

Sarah: *"I appreciate that you're willing to try this. I hope it helps us communicate better. Sometimes I struggle to say things out loud, but maybe writing will be easier."*

Tom: *"I'm nervous about this, but I want us to be closer. I love you and I'm committed to making our relationship stronger."*

As weeks passed, their entries deepened:

Sarah: *"I felt really seen today when you asked about my project. It meant a lot that you remembered the details I'd mentioned before. It made me realize how much I value your interest in my work."*

Tom: *"I've been reflecting on our argument about finances. I realize I get defensive because money was always a stress in my family growing up. I'm working on separating those old fears from our current situation."*

The shared journal became a safe space for vulnerable conversations, helping Sarah and Tom understand each other on a deeper level.

GRATITUDE JOURNALING IN RELATIONSHIPS

Emily and Zoe, married for 15 years, felt their relationship had fallen into a rut. On their anniversary, they decided to start gratitude journals focused on their relationship.

Emily's entry: *"Today I'm grateful for:*

1. *The way Zoe always makes my coffee just right*
2. *Her patience when I'm stressed about work*
3. *The sound of her laugh during our favorite TV show"*

Zoe's entry: *"Grateful for:*

1. *Emily's encouraging text during my tough meeting*
2. *The way she knows when I need a hug without asking*
3. *Her dedication to our garden, which brings beauty to our home"*

As they shared their entries each evening, Emily and Zoe found themselves noticing and appreciating the small moments they had been taking for granted. The practice reignited a spark of romance and deepened their appreciation for each other.

FAMILY JOURNALING: CREATING A SHARED NARRATIVE

The Martinez family - parents Elena and Miguel, and teenagers Sophia and Diego - felt disconnected in the chaos of their busy lives. Inspired by a family therapy session, they started a family journal.

They placed it in the kitchen, agreeing to write at least twice a week and read it together on Sunday evenings. The entries showed a wide variety:

Elena: *"Proud of how we all pitched in to help Abuela move this weekend. This family's strength is in how we support each other."*

Miguel: *"Struggling with work stress this week. Grateful for the understanding and extra help around the house."*

Sophia: *"Can we plan a movie night soon? Miss spending time together without phones and distractions."*

Diego: *"Thanks for coming to my game, even though we lost. It meant a lot to see you all there."*

The family journal became a touchstone, helping them stay connected despite busy schedules and providing a platform for voicing needs and appreciation.

JOURNALING THROUGH RELATIONSHIP CHALLENGES

When Mark and David hit a rough patch in their relationship, their therapist suggested individual journaling as a tool for processing emotions and enhancing their couples therapy.

Mark's journal: *"I'm scared. The distance between us feels vast. But when I think about life without David, it's unimaginable. How did we get here? More importantly, how do we find our way back?"*

David's journal: *"Anger has been my go-to emotion lately, but under-*

neath, I'm hurt. I miss the easy companionship we used to have. I want that back, but I don't know how to bridge this gap."

In therapy sessions, Mark and David used insights from their journals to guide discussions, leading to breakthroughs in their communication and understanding of each other.

THE SCIENCE OF RELATIONSHIP JOURNALING

Recent studies have highlighted the benefits of journaling for relationships:

- A 2019 study in the Journal of Social and Personal Relationships found that couples who engaged in shared journaling reported higher levels of intimacy and relationship satisfaction compared to a control group.
- Research published in Psychological Science in 2020 demonstrated that gratitude journaling focused on one's partner led to increased relationship commitment and pro-relationship behaviors.
- A 2021 study in the journal Family Process showed that families who maintained a shared journal reported improved communication and family cohesion over 6 months.

NAVIGATING PRIVACY AND SHARING IN RELATIONSHIP JOURNALING

As journaling practices intertwine with relationships, questions of privacy naturally arise. Jack and Emma, dating for two years, grappled with this as they explored journaling together.

Jack: *"I want to be open with Emma, but some thoughts feel too raw to share immediately. How do I balance honesty with self-protection?"*

Emma: *"Reading Jack's entries sometimes triggers my insecurities. But it also helps me understand him better. It's a double-edged sword."*

They developed a system:

1. Maintain individual, private journals for unfiltered thoughts
2. Share entries in their couple's journal when ready to discuss
3. Respect each other's privacy and right to keep some thoughts personal
4. Use shared entries as starting points for deeper conversations, not as substitutes for communication

This balanced approach allowed for personal reflection and shared growth, enhancing their relationship without sacrificing individual emotional processing.

INTEGRATING JOURNALING INTO RELATIONSHIP ROUTINES

As Sarah and Tom, Emily and Zoe, the Martinez family, Mark and David, and Jack and Emma continued their journaling practices, they discovered key insights:

1. **Consistency is Key**: Regular entries, even if brief, maintain the practice and its benefits.
2. **Flexibility Matters**: Adapting the journaling style to fit the relationship's current needs enhances its effectiveness.
3. **Non-Judgmental Approach**: Cultivating curiosity rather than judgment when reading shared entries fosters openness and understanding.
4. **Complement, Don't Replace**: Journaling enhances face-to-face communication but doesn't substitute for it.
5. **Celebrate Growth**: Periodically reviewing: Reviewing old

entries together on a regular basis, highlights positive changes and progress in the relationship.

6. **Respect Boundaries**: Honoring individual privacy needs within shared journaling practices builds trust.

Sarah reflected in her personal journal:

"Six months ago, I felt like Tom and I were drifting apart. Now, through our shared journal, I feel more connected than ever. It's not always easy to be vulnerable on the page, but it's opening up conversations we might never have had otherwise. Our relationship feels deeper and more resilient. Who knew that writing could bring us so close?"

As you explore journaling in your own relationships, remember the experiences of these couples and families. Whether you're using individual journals for self-reflection, sharing a couple's journal for deeper connection, or creating a family narrative together, journaling can be a powerful tool for enhancing understanding, fostering appreciation, and navigating challenges.

Your journal is more than a personal record; it can be a bridge to deeper, more fulfilling relationships. What new connections will you forge, one page at a time?

TWENTY-ONE
ETHICAL CONSIDERATIONS IN JOURNALING

Maya's finger hovered over the "Publish" button. Her latest blog post, drawn from her personal journal entries, felt raw and honest. It detailed her struggle with anxiety and how journaling had helped her cope. But as she prepared to share her story with the world, a nagging doubt crept in. Had she considered all the implications?

PRIVACY IN THE DIGITAL AGE

Across town, Alex stared at his phone, his heart racing. He'd just discovered that his cloud storage had been hacked. Somewhere out there, a stranger now had access to years of his most private thoughts and reflections. He'd always considered his digital journal a safe space, but now he felt exposed, vulnerable.

Alex's experience highlighted a crucial issue in modern journaling: digital privacy. As he grappled with the aftermath, he decided to reassess his journaling practice:

1. He researched secure, encrypted journaling apps.
2. He began backing up his entries on an external hard drive, disconnected from the internet.
3. He developed a system of code words for especially sensitive topics.

But most importantly, Alex started each entry with a reminder to himself:

"Remember: Write as if someone might read this someday. Be honest but be mindful."

This new approach didn't diminish the value of his journaling. Instead, it made Alex more intentional about what he wrote and why.

JOURNALING ABOUT OTHERS: THE ETHICS OF STORYTELLING

Emma closed her journal with a sigh. She'd just written a detailed entry about a conflict with her best friend, Sarah. The writing had helped her process her feelings, but now she felt a twinge of guilt. Had she been fair in her portrayal of Sarah? What if Sarah ever read this?

Grappling with this dilemma, Emma developed a new approach to writing about others:

1. She focused on her own feelings and reactions rather than making judgments about others' motivations.
2. She used initials instead of full names when writing about sensitive situations.
3. When describing conflicts, she challenged herself to consider the other person's perspective.

Emma's next entry reflected this new mindset:

"Had a disagreement with S. today. I felt hurt when she canceled our plans last minute. My initial reaction was anger - I thought she was being inconsiderate. But stepping back, I wonder if something else is going on with her. Maybe she's dealing with stress that I don't know about. Next time, I'll try to ask her how she's doing before jumping to conclusions."

This approach allowed Emma to maintain the therapeutic benefits of journaling while being more ethical and empathetic in her reflections on others.

CULTURAL SENSITIVITY IN JOURNALING PRACTICES

Jamal's pen raced across the page as he recorded his experiences studying abroad in Japan. He described the "weird" foods he'd tried, the "crazy" customs he'd observed, the "backward" way of doing things. It wasn't until he reread his entries weeks later that he realized how his words might come across.

Embarrassed by his lack of cultural sensitivity, Jamal decided to transform his journaling practice:

1. He started each entry by acknowledging that he was viewing things through the lens of his own cultural background.
2. He challenged himself to find the logic or value in customs different from his own.
3. He focused on describing experiences without bias before adding his personal reactions.

Jamal's later entries showed a marked shift:

"Attended a tea ceremony today. At first, the precise movements and long silences felt strange to me - I'm used to more casual, chatty gatherings. However, as I observed more closely, I began to appreciate the mindfulness of each action. It made me reflect on how rushed and distracted I often am

during social interactions back home. There's a beauty to this intention-ality that I hadn't considered before."

Through this more mindful approach, Jamal's journal became a tool not just for recording experiences, but for personal growth and cultural understanding.

THE IMPACT OF JOURNALING ON MENTAL HEALTH: RESPONSIBLE SELF-REFLECTION

Dr. Lena Warren, a psychologist, often recommended journaling to her patients. However as she reviewed her case notes one evening, she realized the practice wasn't beneficial for everyone. Some patients seemed to spiral into negativity, their journals becoming a forum for rumination rather than reflection.

Concerned, Dr. Warren developed guidelines for ethical, mentally healthy journaling:

1. Balance negative reflections with positive ones. For every problem noted, try to include a potential solution or silver lining.
2. Set time limits for journaling sessions to prevent excessive rumination.
3. Use journaling as a complement to, not a replacement for, professional help when dealing with serious mental health issues.
4. Review old entries on a regular basis to track patterns and progress.

She shared these guidelines with her patient, Tom, who had been struggling with depression. Tom's next session revealed a shift:

"I've been trying that new journaling approach, Doc. Instead of just vent-ing, I've been challenging myself to find one good thing each day, no

matter how small. Yesterday, I wrote about how the barista remembered my order. Tiny thing, but it made me feel a bit more connected to the world. It's not fixing everything, but I think it's helping me notice the good stuff I was overlooking before."

Dr. Warren's ethical approach to journaling was helping her patients use the practice as a tool for growth rather than a crutch for negative patterns.

JOURNALING AND SOCIAL MEDIA: NAVIGATING PUBLIC VS. PRIVATE EXPRESSION

Zoe's Instagram feed was filled with curated photos of journal pages, inspirational quotes, and intimate reflections. Her "authentic journaling" account had gained thousands of followers, but she had started to feel conflicted about what to share.

As Zoe grappled with the blurred lines between private reflection and public performance, she decided to set some boundaries:

1. She maintained a separate, private journal for her most personal thoughts.
2. Before posting any journal content, she waited 24 hours and reevaluated if she still felt comfortable sharing.
3. She was honest with her followers about the curated nature of what she shared, posting about the less glamorous aspects of journaling.

Zoe's next post reflected this new approach:

"Real talk: Not every journal page is Instagram-worthy. Sometimes it's messy, sometimes it's boring, and sometimes it's too personal to share. And that's okay. Journaling, at its core, is for you - not for likes or followers. Here's to embracing all aspects of the journey, even the parts we don't show online. #AuthenticJournaling #TheFullPicture"

By being more intentional about what she shared, Zoe found a balance between inspiring others and maintaining the integrity of her personal practice.

THE SCIENCE OF ETHICAL JOURNALING

Recent studies have shed light on the ethical considerations in journaling:

- A 2020 study in the Journal of Medical Internet Research found that users of digital journaling apps often underestimated the privacy risks associated with cloud-based storage of personal data.
- Research published in Qualitative Health Research in 2021 explored the ethical implications of using personal journals in academic research, highlighting the need for clear consent processes and anonymization techniques.
- A 2019 study in Computers in Human Behavior demonstrated that social media sharing of journal content was associated with increased self-censorship in private journaling practices, which could reduce the therapeutic benefits.

INTEGRATING ETHICAL CONSIDERATIONS INTO YOUR JOURNALING PRACTICE

As Maya, Alex, Emma, Jamal, Tom, and Zoe navigated the ethical challenges of journaling, they discovered key insights:

1. **Privacy is Paramount**: Whether journaling digitally or on paper, take steps to protect your personal information.
2. **Empathy in Expression**: When writing about others, strive for fairness and consider multiple perspectives.

3. **Cultural Awareness**: Use journaling as a tool for understanding and appreciating cultural differences, not reinforcing stereotypes.
4. **Mental Health Mindfulness**: Balance honest expression with practices that support positive mental health.
5. **Intentional Sharing**: Carefully consider the implications before making private reflections public.
6. **Consent and Anonymity**: If using journal content for public purposes (e.g., writing, research), ensure proper consent and protect the privacy of the individuals mentioned.
7. **Regular Ethical Check-ins**: Periodically: From time to time review your journaling practice to ensure it aligns with your values and respects both yourself and others.

Maya, her finger still hovering over the "Publish" button, took a deep breath. She reread her post, considering the potential impact on herself and others. She made a few thoughtful edits, ensuring she represented everyone fairly and protected private information. Finally, feeling confident in the ethics of her share, she clicked "Publish."

As you continue your journaling journey, remember the experiences of these individuals. Your journal is a powerful tool for self-expression, growth, and understanding. By approaching it with ethical mindfulness, you can ensure that your practice honors both yourself and others.

What new insights will you uncover as you journal with integrity and awareness?

TWENTY-TWO

FROM JOURNAL TO MEMOIR

Eleanor's fingers trembled as she opened the dusty box. Decades of journals lay inside, a treasure trove of memories, reflections, and personal growth. At 65, she'd decided it was time to write her memoir, but where to start? As she lifted out the earliest journal, its pages yellowed with age, she was transported back to her 16-year-old self.

UNEARTHING THE PAST: THE JOURNEY BEGINS

July 15, 1972

Dear Diary,

Mom and Dad are fighting again. I wish I could disappear. Maybe I'll run away to New York and become a famous actress...

Eleanor chuckled at her teenage dramatics but felt a pang of empathy for her younger self. As she continued reading, patterns emerged - dreams, struggles, and pivotal moments that had shaped her life's trajectory.

She grabbed a fresh notebook and began jotting down potential themes for her memoir:

- Family dynamics and their lasting impact
- The pursuit of dreams vs. practical realities
- Navigating love and heartbreak
- Career evolution and personal growth
- Motherhood and identity

With each journal she revisited, Eleanor's vision for her memoir became clearer. This wouldn't just be a chronological retelling of events, but a thematic exploration of her life's journey.

CRAFTING THE NARRATIVE: FROM RAW MATERIAL TO POLISHED PROSE

Mark, a 45-year-old teacher, sat at his desk surrounded by piles of journals. He had maintained a consistent writing practice for over two decades and now felt ready to shape his experiences into a memoir about his journey as an educator.

He opened his laptop and began the daunting task of transforming raw journal entries into a coherent narrative:

Original Journal Entry (September 5, 2005):

Tough first day. The kids were wild. Felt overwhelmed and underprepared. Is this really what I signed up for? Maybe Dad was right, should've gone into accounting...

Memoir Draft:

As I stood before my first class, the cacophony of twenty-eight seventh graders washing over me, I felt the ground shift beneath my feet. This wasn't the inspiring "Dead Poets Society" moment I'd envisioned. It was chaos, pure and simple. In that moment, my father's pragmatic voice echoed in my head: "Teaching? That's a noble profession, son, but have you considered accounting?" I pushed the thought aside, took a deep breath, and picked up the chalk. I had no idea then that this day of doubt would be the first step on a journey that would transform not just my career, but my entire life.

Mark read over his draft, pleased with how he'd expanded the brief journal entry into a more vivid, reflective scene. He realized that the process of writing his memoir wasn't just about recounting events, but about extracting meaning and insight from his experiences.

NAVIGATING SENSITIVE TOPICS: BALANCING HONESTY AND RESPECT

Sarah stared at her journal entry from ten years ago, tears welling in her eyes. It detailed the painful falling out with her sister, a rift that had only recently begun to heal. She knew this event was crucial to her story, but how could she write about it without reopening old wounds?

She decided to approach the topic with care:

1. She wrote a draft focusing on her own emotions and perspective, without assigning blame.
2. She reflected on how the experience had led to personal growth and, eventually, reconciliation.
3. She decided to share the draft with her sister before including it in the memoir, valuing their renewed relationship over literary revelation.

Sarah's resulting memoir passage struck a balance between honesty and sensitivity:

The day my sister and I stopped speaking was the day I learned that love and hurt can coexist in equal measure. Our words, sharp as knives, left wounds that would take years to heal. But in the silence that followed, I began to understand the complexities of family, forgiveness, and the long road back to each other. This chapter of our lives, painful as it was, ultimately taught us both the value of compassion and the strength found in vulnerability.

RESEARCH AND FACT-CHECKING: ENHANCING MEMORY WITH HISTORICAL CONTEXT

James, a 70-year-old veteran, had kept journals throughout his military service. As he worked on his memoir, he realized that his personal experiences were intertwined with significant historical events. Determined to provide an accurate account, he embarked on a journey of research and fact-checking.

For a pivotal chapter about his time in Vietnam, James:

1. Cross-referenced his journal dates with historical records of military operations.
2. Interviewed fellow veterans to corroborate shared experiences.
3. Visited his local library to access newspapers from the period.
4. Consulted with a military historian to ensure accuracy in his descriptions of equipment and procedures.

This process not only enhanced the historical accuracy of his memoir but also brought new insights into his own memories. James's resulting chapter wove personal experience with historical context:

As our helicopter descended toward the village, the date etched in my mind - March 16, 1968 - I had no idea we were about to become part of a dark chapter in military history. My journal entry that night was brief: "Heavy firefight. Civilian casualties. Something feels wrong." It would be years before I understood the full context of what transpired in My Lai that day, and how it would haunt not just me, but the entire nation's conscience.

THE ART OF SELECTIVITY: CHOOSING WHAT TO INCLUDE AND WHAT TO LEAVE OUT

Elena, a 55-year-old artist, felt overwhelmed by the sheer volume of material in her journals. Decades of daily entries, sketches, and reflections - how could she possibly distill this into a coherent memoir?

She developed a system:

1. She created a timeline of key life events and turning points.
2. She identified recurring themes and motifs in her journals.
3. She selected entries that best illustrated these themes or provided unique insights.
4. She made the difficult decision to focus on her artistic journey, leaving out many personal anecdotes.

Elena's selective approach resulted in a memoir that was focused and thematically rich, tracing her evolution as an artist while still providing glimpses into her personal life:

The first time I held a brush, I was four years old. The last time, as of writing this, was an hour ago. In between those moments lies a lifetime of color, form, triumph, and doubt. This memoir is not a comprehensive account of my days, but rather a palette of moments that, when combined, paint the picture of an artist's journey - from the first tentative strokes to the confident sweeps of a hand that has learned to trust its own vision.

THE IMPACT OF MEMOIR WRITING: PERSONAL GROWTH AND SHARED HUMAN EXPERIENCE

As Eleanor, Mark, Sarah, James, and Elena worked on their memoirs, they discovered that the process was transformative not just for their writing, but for their understanding of themselves and their lives.

Eleanor found herself forgiving her younger self for mistakes she'd long regretted. Mark gained a deeper appreciation for his teaching career and the impact he'd had on students' lives. Sarah's work on her memoir facilitated deeper healing and communication with her sister. James's research brought a new perspective to his military experiences. Elena saw her artistic journey with fresh eyes, recognizing patterns of growth she hadn't noticed before.

However, the impact extended beyond personal growth. As they shared drafts with trusted readers, they found that their stories resonated in unexpected ways. Mark's struggles as a new teacher inspired a young educator to persevere. Sarah's account of reconciliation with her sister gave hope to a friend amid a family conflict. James's memoir provided insight into the veteran experience for readers who had never served.

THE SCIENCE OF MEMOIR WRITING

Recent studies have highlighted the benefits of transforming journal entries into memoirs:

- A 2019 study in the Journal of Personality and Social Psychology found that individuals who engaged in structured autobiographical writing showed increased self-awareness and reported a greater sense of personal growth compared to a control group.
- Research published in Narrative Inquiry in 2020 demonstrated that the process of selecting and

contextualizing journal entries for memoir writing led to new insights and reinterpretations of past events, contributing to enhanced psychological well-being.

- A 2021 study in the journal Memory found that the act of writing a memoir enhanced autobiographical memory specificity, which is associated with improved problem-solving skills and reduced depressive symptoms.

FROM PRIVATE REFLECTIONS TO PUBLIC NARRATIVE: EMBRACING VULNERABILITY

As Eleanor put the finishing touches on her memoir manuscript, she felt a mix of excitement and trepidation. Sharing her life story with the world was daunting, but she reminded herself of the power of shared human experience.

She wrote in her current journal:

"As I prepare to send my memoir out into the world, I'm struck by how this process has transformed my relationship with my journals. What once were private repositories of my innermost thoughts have become a bridge - not just between my past and present selves, but between my experiences and those of others. I've learned that our most personal stories, when shared with authenticity and vulnerability, have the power to connect us all."

Eleanor closed her journal, took a deep breath, and turned to her computer to compose the email that would send her manuscript to her editor. Her journey from journal to memoir was nearing its end, but in many ways, it felt like a new beginning.

As you consider your own journals and the possibility of shaping them into a larger narrative, remember the experiences of Eleanor, Mark, Sarah, James, and Elena. Your journal entries are more than just daily records - they're the raw material of your life story, filled with insights, growth, and shared human experiences waiting to be explored.

Whether you're looking to publish a full memoir or simply want to gain a deeper understanding of your own journey, the process of revisiting and reshaping your journal entries can be profoundly rewarding. What hidden chapters of your life are waiting to be discovered in the pages of your journals?

TWENTY-THREE
EMERGING TRENDS IN JOURNALING

Zoe stared at her smartphone, thumb hovering over an app icon shaped like a quill. She'd been keeping a paper journal for years, but her friend had raved about this new AI-assisted journaling app. With a mix of curiosity and apprehension, she tapped the icon and began her journey into the future of journaling.

AI-ASSISTED JOURNALING: A NEW FRONTIER

As Zoe typed her first entry, she noticed something unusual. The app wasn't just passively recording her thoughts; it was actively engaging with them:

Zoe: "Feeling stuck at work lately. Not sure if I should look for a new job or try to make changes where I am."

AI Assistant: "It sounds like you're at a career crossroads. Have you considered making a list of what you enjoy about your current job and what you'd like to change? This might help clarify your thoughts."

Intrigued, Zoe followed the suggestion. As she listed her job satisfactions and frustrations, the AI offered more prompts:

AI Assistant: "I notice you mentioned 'lack of creative opportunities' as a frustration. Can you think of any ways to incorporate more creativity into your current role?"

This AI-guided introspection led Zoe to insights she might not have reached on her own. She realized that while she loved her team and the company's mission, she craved more creative challenges. This clarity inspired her to draft a proposal for a new project that would align her role with her passions.

As the weeks passed, Zoe found the AI's prompts increasingly tailored to her writing style and concerns. It noted patterns in her mood and gently suggested reflection on recurring themes. While skeptical at first, Zoe found that this AI-human collaboration deepened her journaling practice in unexpected ways.

INTEGRATION WITH PRODUCTIVITY TOOLS: JOURNALING IN THE FLOW OF LIFE

Across town, Alex, a project manager, was exploring a different journaling frontier. He'd always struggled to maintain a consistent journaling habit, finding it disconnected from his daily workflow. Then he discovered an integration between his project management software and a journaling app.

Now, at the end of each workday, a notification prompted Alex to reflect on his progress:

Project Management Software: "You completed the client presentation ahead of schedule. How do you feel about this achievement?"

Alex: "Relieved and proud. The team really came together on this one. I think the new collaboration process we implemented made a big difference."

Software: "That's great! Would you like to expand on how the new collaboration process contributed to this success?"

This seamless integration allowed Alex to capture insights about his work and personal growth without switching contexts. He found himself more mindful of his daily experiences and better able to track his professional development over time.

The app also allowed Alex to tag entries with project names or skills, creating a searchable database of his professional journey. When preparing for his annual review, Alex could easily pull up relevant reflections, providing concrete examples of his growth and contributions.

VOICE AND VIDEO JOURNALING: CAPTURING THE FULLNESS OF EXPERIENCE

Maya, a travel blogger, had always found traditional journaling too time-consuming while on the road. But when she discovered a new app that combined voice recognition, video recording, and automatic transcription, her journaling practice was transformed.

While exploring a bustling market in Marrakech, Maya simply tapped her smartwatch and began narrating:

"The air is thick with the scent of spices - cumin, saffron, cinnamon. A vendor just offered me a sip of mint tea, served in a delicate glass with intricate patterns. The warmth of the tea and the vendor's smile make me feel welcomed in this sea of sensory overload."

Later that evening, Maya found a transcription of her voice notes in her journaling app, alongside the video clips she'd recorded. The app had even generated tags based on her content: #Morocco #MarrakechMarket #CulinaryExperiences.

This multimedia approach allowed Maya to capture the vibrancy of her travels in a way that written words alone never could. The combination of her spoken thoughts, visual memories, and the app's organization features created a rich, multidimensional journal that brought her experiences to life.

GAMIFICATION OF JOURNALING: BUILDING LASTING HABITS

Tom had always admired people who journaled on a consistent basis, but he could never seem to stick with it himself. That changed when he discovered an app that turned journaling into a game.

The app sets daily challenges:

- *"Write about a small victory you had today. (+10 points)"*
- *"Reflect on a mistake and what you learned from it. (+15 points)"*
- *"Describe your current surroundings using all five senses. (+20 points)"*

As Tom completed challenges, he earned points, unlocked new features, and watched his "Reflection Level" rise. The app also had a social component, allowing users to share selected entries (anonymously if desired) and support each other's journaling streaks.

What started as a fun diversion quickly became a meaningful practice for Tom. The gamification elements motivated him to maintain a consistent writing practice, while the varied prompts encouraged him to explore different aspects of his life and mindset.

Three months in, Tom realized he'd journaled every day without fail - a personal record. More importantly, he'd developed a deeper understanding of himself and his goals. The game had become a gateway to genuine self-reflection.

THE SCIENCE BEHIND NEW JOURNALING TECHNOLOGIES

Recent studies have begun to explore the impact of these emerging journaling trends:

- A 2023 study published in the Journal of Computer-Mediated Communication found that users of AI-assisted journaling apps reported higher levels of self-insight and emotional clarity compared to traditional journalers.
- Research from the University of California in 2024 demonstrated that integration of journaling with productivity tools led to improved work satisfaction and clearer goal-setting among professionals.
- A 2025 study in the journal Computers in Human Behavior showed that multimedia journaling (combining text, voice, and video) enhanced memory recall and emotional processing of experiences, with greater benefits for individuals with visual or auditory processing preferences.
- The Journal of Positive Psychology published a study in 2024 indicating that gamified journaling apps increased user engagement and consistency, with participants showing significant improvements in well-being metrics over 6 months.

NAVIGATING THE FUTURE OF JOURNALING

As Zoe, Alex, Maya, and Tom explored these new frontiers in journaling, they discovered both exciting possibilities and important considerations:

1. **Personalization is Key**: The most effective new journaling tools adapt to individual preferences and needs.
2. **Privacy Matters**: With increased digital integration comes

the need for robust security measures to protect personal reflections.

3. **Balance Technology and Mindfulness**: While new tools can enhance the journaling experience, it's important to maintain the mindful, reflective nature of the practice.

4. **Embrace Flexibility**: The best journaling practice combines elements that work for the individual, whether high-tech or traditional.

5. **Stay Curious**: As new journaling technologies emerge, an open and experimental mindset can lead to discovering beneficial practices.

Zoe reflected on her journey into AI-assisted journaling:

"When I first started using this app, I was worried it might make journaling feel artificial. Instead, it's like having a thoughtful friend who asks just the right questions to help me dig deeper. It hasn't replaced my traditional journaling—sometimes I still crave the feel of pen on paper. But it's added a new dimension to my self-reflection practice. I'm excited to see how journaling will continue to evolve, and how I'll evolve with it."

As you consider your own journaling practice, remember the experiences of Zoe, Alex, Maya, and Tom. The future of journaling offers a wealth of new tools and approaches, each with the potential to enhance your self-reflection and personal growth in unique ways.

Whether you're drawn to AI-assisted insights, seamless integration with your digital life, multimedia expression, or motivating game elements, the key is to find the methods that resonate with you. The essence of journaling—honest self-expression and reflection—remains the same, even as the tools we use continue to evolve.

What new journaling frontiers will you explore, and how might they deepen your understanding of yourself and your world?

TWENTY-FOUR
BUILDING A JOURNALING COMMUNITY

Sarah's hand trembled slightly as she pushed open the door to the local community center. The handmade sign read "Journaling Circle - All Welcome!" She clutched her well-worn notebook to her chest, excitement and nerves battling within her. After years of solitary journaling, she was about to share her practice with others for the first time.

STARTING A JOURNALING GROUP: FROM SOLO PRACTICE TO SHARED EXPERIENCE

Inside, a circle of chairs awaited. Sarah recognized a few faces - her neighbor Tom, the barista from her favorite coffee shop, and her stoic dentist, Dr. Wade. As more people filtered in, the room hummed with a mix of anticipation and uncertainty.

Sarah cleared her throat and began, "Welcome, everyone. I'm so glad you're here. I thought we could start by sharing what brought us to journaling..."

As stories unfolded, Sarah realized she had tapped into a hidden need in her community. Tom spoke of using journaling to process his grief after losing his wife. The barista, Jade, described how writing helped her manage anxiety. Dr. Wade admitted that journaling was his secret tool for work-life balance.

Over the weeks, the group developed its own rhythm:

1. They started each session with a brief meditation to center themselves.
2. Sarah introduced a prompt or theme for those who wanted guidance.
3. They wrote for 20 minutes, the room filled only with the sound of pens scratching paper.
4. Afterward, members could choose to share a snippet of their writing or a reflection on the process.
5. They closed with a gratitude circle, each person naming one thing they appreciated about the session.

As the group bonded, they began to explore different journaling techniques together. One week, they experimented with stream-of-consciousness writing. Another, they tried art journaling, the table strewn with colored pencils and magazines for collage.

Sarah watched in awe as the shy teenager, Alex, blossomed in confidence, his poetic words earning supportive snaps from the group. She saw unlikely friendships form, like the one between the retired teacher and the young entrepreneur, bonding over their shared love of list-making in their journals.

ONLINE JOURNALING COMMUNITIES: CONNECTING ACROSS DISTANCES

Meanwhile, halfway across the country, Marcus stared at his

computer screen, cursor blinking in the search bar. "Journaling forums," he typed, hoping to find kindred spirits in the digital realm.

He stumbled upon a vibrant online community called "InkWell." After creating a profile, Marcus found himself immersed in a world of fellow journal enthusiasts:

- The "Daily Prompt" thread buzzed with responses to thought-provoking questions.
- In "Technique Talk," members shared tips on everything from bullet journaling to mindfulness writing.
- The "Journal Showcase" forum was a gallery of inspirational spreads and creative layouts.
- A "Motivation Station" board offered support for those struggling to maintain their practice.

Marcus tentatively made his first post:

"New here. Been journaling for years but feeling stuck lately. Any advice for rekindling the spark?"

Within hours, his post was flooded with encouraging responses:

"Welcome, Marcus! Have you tried changing up your journaling environment? Sometimes a new location can inspire fresh thoughts." - JournalJunkie

"When I'm in a rut, I love to try a new journaling method. Maybe give the 'Unsent Letter' technique a go?" - PenAndSoul

"Sending motivation your way! Remember, even a sentence a day keeps the journaling flow alive." - WordsFlow

Marcus felt a weight lift from his shoulders. He wasn't alone in his struggles, and a world of new possibilities had just opened up to him.

As he engaged more with the community, Marcus found himself trying new techniques, participating in journaling challenges, and even mentoring newcomers. His solitary practice had transformed into a rich, collaborative experience.

JOURNALING WORKSHOPS AND RETREATS: IMMERSIVE LEARNING EXPERIENCES

Elena smoothed her shirt as she stood before the group of eager faces. The sign behind her read "Journaling for Self-Discovery: A Weekend Retreat." Months of planning had led to this moment.

"Welcome, everyone," she began. "Over the next two days, we'll be diving deep into the transformative power of journaling. But first, let's start with a simple check-in. Please take a moment to write down how you're feeling right now, using only three words."

As pens hit paper, Elena felt the energy in the room shift. The retreat unfolded in a carefully crafted sequence:

1. **Day 1 Morning**: Exploring different journaling styles (free writing, structured prompts, gratitude journaling)
2. **Day 1 Afternoon**: Nature walk with sensory journaling exercise
3. **Day 1 Evening**: Reflective journaling by candlelight, focusing on life goals and values
4. **Day 2 Morning**: Art journaling workshop, encouraging visual expression
5. **Day 2 Afternoon**: Peer sharing circles and collaborative journaling exercises
6. **Day 2 Evening**: Crafting personal journaling rituals and setting future intentions

Throughout the retreat, Elena watched transformations unfold. The stressed-out executive who arrived with slumped shoulders was now standing taller, eyes bright with new insights. The quiet artist who barely spoke on day one was now sharing her stunning illustrated journal pages.

In the closing circle, participants shared their experiences:

"I've been journaling for years, but I never realized how much deeper I could go. This weekend has been revelatory." - Michael, 52

"I came here skeptical, thinking journaling was just for writers. Now I see it's for everyone. I can't wait to continue this practice at home." - Amira, 29

"The combination of solo reflection and group sharing was powerful. I feel like I understand myself better, and I've made connections I'll cherish." - Luis, 41

As the retreat ended, Elena felt a deep sense of fulfillment. She had created a space for people to connect with themselves and each other through the power of journaling.

THE SCIENCE OF COMMUNAL JOURNALING

Recent studies have begun to explore the benefits of shared journaling experiences:

- A 2023 study in the Journal of Community Psychology found that participants in regular journaling groups reported increased feelings of social connection and improved emotional well-being compared to solo journalers.
- Research published in Computers in Human Behavior in 2024 showed that active participation in online journaling communities was associated with increased journaling consistency and greater perceived benefits from the practice.

- A 2025 study in the Journal of Experiential Education demonstrated that immersive journaling retreats led to significant short-term increases in self-awareness and life satisfaction, with effects persisting at a 3-month follow-up.

NURTURING A THRIVING JOURNALING COMMUNITY

As Sarah, Marcus, and Elena fostered their respective journaling communities, they discovered key insights:

1. **Create Safe Spaces**: Establishing clear guidelines for respect and confidentiality is crucial for open sharing.
2. **Embrace Diversity**: A mix of ages, backgrounds, and journaling styles enriches the community experience.
3. **Balance Structure and Freedom**: Provide prompts and guidance but allow room for individual expression.
4. **Encourage Cross-Pollination**: Facilitate the sharing of techniques and insights among members.
5. **Evolve with Your Community**: Be open to adjusting formats and activities based on group feedback and needs.
6. **Extend Beyond Meetings**: Encourage connections between sessions through social media groups or buddy systems.
7. **Celebrate Milestones**: Acknowledge both individual and group achievements in journaling practice.

Sarah reflected on her journaling group's six-month anniversary:

"When I started this group, I thought I was just creating a space to share our writing. What we've built is a supportive family, a place where we can be our authentic selves. Watching each member grow, including myself, has been the most rewarding experience. Our journals aren't just personal records anymore; they're threads in a beautiful communal tapestry we're weaving together."

As you consider your own journaling practice, remember the experiences of Sarah, Marcus, and Elena. Journaling doesn't have to be a solitary pursuit. By connecting with others who share your passion, you can deepen your practice, gain new perspectives, and find support on your journey of self-discovery.

Whether you join a local group, engage in online communities, or attend immersive retreats, remember that the heart of communal journaling is shared growth and connection. Your unique voice and experiences are valuable contributions to the collective wisdom of your journaling community.

What new horizons might you discover by sharing your journaling journey with others?

APPENDIX A: JOURNALING PROMPTS FOR EVERY OCCASION

DAILY REFLECTION PROMPTS

1. The Highlight Reel

Prompt: What was the highlight of your day, and why did it stand out?

Example Entry:

"Today's highlight was definitely the impromptu picnic in the park with Sarah. We were supposed to grab a quick lunch, but the weather was so perfect we decided to buy sandwiches and eat outside. The sun on my face, the light breeze, and Sarah's contagious laughter as we people-watched — it all combined to create this perfect bubble of joy. It reminded me how important it is to seize these spontaneous moments of happiness."

2. Challenge Accepted

Prompt: Describe a challenge you faced today. How did you handle it, and what did you learn?

Example Entry:

"The client presentation didn't go as smoothly as I'd hoped. Our main competitor had just launched a similar product, which threw a wrench in our pitch. In that moment, I felt my stomach drop, but I took a deep breath and addressed it head-on. I talked about how our product differed and why ours was superior. The clients seemed impressed by the quick thinking. Lesson learned: Always be prepared for curveballs, and don't be afraid to tackle them directly."

3. Gratitude Check-In

Prompt: List three things you're grateful for today. Try to be specific and avoid repetition from previous days.

Example Entry:

1. *The barista who remembered my complicated coffee order and had it ready before I even reached the counter. That small gesture made me feel seen and appreciated.*
2. *The vibrant red of the autumn leaves on my walk home. Nature's beauty is such a simple yet profound joy.*
3. *My old college roommate texting to check in, just because. It's comforting to know that some friendships remain strong despite time and distance."*

SELF-DISCOVERY PROMPTS

1. Values Exploration

Prompt: Reflect on a recent decision you made. What personal values did it reflect?

Example Entry:

"I've been thinking about my decision to turn down that job offer last month. On paper, it looked great — more money, prestigious company. But something felt off. As I reflect, I realize this decision really highlighted my value of work-life balance. The new job would have meant longer hours

and more travel, taking me away from my family and my hobbies. By choosing to stay at my current job, I'm honoring my belief that success isn't just about career advancement or money, but about building a well-rounded, fulfilling life."

2. **The Skill Master**

Prompt: If you could instantly master one skill, what would it be and how would it change your life?

Example Entry:

"If I could instantly master one skill, it would be playing the piano. I can imagine my fingers flying over the keys, bringing beautiful melodies to life. This skill would add a new dimension to my life – a way to express emotions when words fail, a method to relax and de-stress after a long day. I'd love to play at family gatherings, and maybe even compose my own music. It would be a bridge to connect with others who love music, opening up a whole new community. Most importantly, it would be a reminder that it's never too late to learn something new and find joy in the process of creation."

3. **A Day in the Ideal Life**

Prompt: Describe your ideal day from start to finish. Be as detailed as possible.

Example Entry:

"I wake up naturally as sunlight filters through the curtains. No alarm needed – I've had a restful 8 hours of sleep. I start with a short meditation, followed by yoga on my balcony overlooking the ocean. Breakfast is a leisurely affair – fresh fruit, whole grain toast, and perfectly brewed coffee.

I spend the morning working on my novel, the words flowing easily. My creativity feels boundless. Lunch is a healthy salad, eaten mindfully away from any screens.

The afternoon is split between a walk in nature and volunteering at the local animal shelter. Both activities fill me with a sense of purpose and connection.

In the evening, I cook a delicious, nutritious meal with my partner. We eat on the patio, sharing stories about our day. The night ends with reading a good book, feeling satisfied with a day well-lived, excited for what tomorrow might bring."

EMOTIONAL EXPLORATION PROMPTS

1. **Joy Journal**

Prompt: Recall a moment of pure joy. Describe it in vivid detail – what did you see, hear, smell, taste, feel?

Example Entry:

"It was my nephew's 5th birthday party. The moment that stands out is when we brought out the cake. His eyes went wide, reflecting the flickering candles. The room filled with the warm, sweet scent of chocolate and the sound of off-key but enthusiastic singing.

As we finished the song, he closed his eyes tight, his face scrunched in concentration before blowing out the candles. When he opened them, his smile was so bright it could have lit the room on its own. He looked at me and shouted, "I did it, Auntie!"

In that moment, I felt a surge of love so strong it was almost overwhelming. My cheeks hurt from smiling, my heart felt full to bursting. It was pure, unadulterated joy – the kind that makes you grateful to be alive and present in that exact moment."

2. **Fear Factor**

Prompt: What fear is holding you back? Imagine your life if you overcame it. What would change?

Example Entry:

"The fear of public speaking has been holding me back. It's why I've turned down opportunities to present at conferences, and why I shy away from leading meetings at work. If I overcame this fear... wow, the possibilities seem endless.

I imagine confidently standing on a stage, sharing my ideas with a captivated audience. At work, I'd be able to articulate my thoughts more clearly in meetings, potentially leading to faster career advancement.

Beyond work, I might join a local Toastmasters group, expanding my social circle. I could even use these skills to advocate for causes I care about in my community.

Overcoming this fear would be like removing a barrier that's been holding me back in so many areas of life. It's not just about speaking — it's about having the confidence to share my voice with the world."

3. Letter to Your Younger Self

Prompt: Write a letter to your younger self (choose a specific age). What advice or comfort would you offer?

Example Entry:

"Dear 16-year-old me,

I know you're struggling right now. High school feels like it's everything, but I promise you, it's just a small part of your journey. Those friends who seem so important? Some will stay in your life, others will drift away, and that's okay. You'll meet so many amazing people in the years to come.

That dream of becoming a writer that you're too scared to talk about? Hold onto it. It's not an impossible fantasy. You have talent, and with hard work, you'll make it happen. Don't let anyone tell you it's not a "real" career.

I know you worry about finding love. Stop. The right person will come along when you least expect it. Focus on loving yourself first

Most importantly, be kinder to yourself. Those perceived flaws that you obsess over? They're part of what makes you unique. Embrace them

You're stronger than you know, smarter than you give yourself credit for, and have so much potential. Trust yourself. The best is yet to come

Love,

Your future self"

Remember, these are just starting points. Let the prompts guide you, but don't feel constrained by them. Your journal is a space for your authentic thoughts and feelings, wherever they may lead you. Happy journaling!

APPENDIX B: SAMPLE JOURNAL ENTRIES

1. STREAM OF CONSCIOUSNESS ENTRY

Date: July 15, 2025

Time: 6:45 AM

Location: My bedroom desk

"Just woke up head still fuzzy from that weird dream can't quite remember it but there was a purple elephant I think why am I thinking about elephants need coffee the sun is so bright today maybe I should go for a walk later but first that report for work ugh don't want to think about it now but it's due tomorrow procrastinated too long again why do I always do this to myself remember to call Mom it's her birthday next week what should I get her she always says she doesn't need anything but I want to get her something special maybe a cooking class she's been talking about trying new recipes lately or maybe that book she mentioned last month what was it called something about gardening in small spaces I should write it down before I forget again oh no I'm going to be late for work if I

don't start getting ready now but I'm so comfortable here just five more minutes..."

Tip: Don't censor yourself during stream-of-consciousness writing. Let your thoughts flow, no matter how random or disconnected they may seem. This technique can help uncover subconscious thoughts and feelings.

2. GRATITUDE JOURNAL ENTRY

Date: August 3, 2025

Today, I am grateful for:

1. The cool breeze that swept through the city this morning, bringing relief from the heatwave we've been experiencing. The way it made the leaves dance on the trees outside my window was mesmerizing.

2. My best friend Alex's unwavering support. He listened to me vent about work for an hour last night and somehow managed to make me laugh by the end of the call. True friendship is a rare and precious gift.

3. The small urban garden I've managed to create on my balcony. Seeing the first tomato ripen on the vine fills me with an inexplicable sense of accomplishment and connection to nature.

4. The barista at my local coffee shop who always remembers my order and asks about my day. These small, genuine interactions make me feel seen and appreciated in this big, busy city.

5. My health. After witnessing a colleague's struggle with a chronic illness, I'm reminded not to take my well-being for granted. The simple ability to take a deep breath or go for a run is truly a blessing.

Tip: Try to be specific in your gratitude entries. Instead of just writing "I'm grateful for my job," detail a particular aspect or event from work that you appreciate.

3. GOAL-SETTING JOURNAL ENTRY

Date: January 1, 2026

This year, I want to focus on three main goals:

1. Health: Run a half-marathon

Why: To challenge myself physically and prove that I can achieve something I once thought impossible.

Action steps:

- *Research and sign up for a half-marathon in October*
- *Download a training app and start a 6-month training plan by April 1st*
- *Join a local running group for motivation and support*
- *Gradually adjust my diet to support my training (more whole foods, less processed stuff)*
- *Invest in proper running shoes and gear by February*

2. Career: Transition into a leadership role

Why: To grow professionally and have a greater impact on my team and company.

Action steps:

- *Schedule a meeting with my manager to discuss my career aspirations*
- *Identify and take on two high-visibility projects in Q1*
- *Enroll in a leadership development course by March*
- *Find a mentor in a leadership position by April*
- *Read one leadership book per month and apply key learnings*

3. Personal: Learn to speak conversational Spanish

Why: To challenge my brain, connect with a new culture, and prepare for my dream trip to Spain.

Action steps:

- *Download a language learning app and practice for 20 minutes daily*
- *Find a language exchange partner by February*
- *Watch one Spanish movie or TV show episode per week with subtitles*
- *Attend a local Spanish conversation group twice a month*
- *Plan a two-week immersion trip to Spain for December*

Remember: Progress, not perfection. Celebrate small wins along the way!

Tip: Break down your goals into smaller, actionable steps. This makes them less overwhelming and easier to achieve. Establish a routine to review and adjust your goals as needed.

4. REFLECTIVE JOURNAL ENTRY

Date: September 10, 2026

Had a tough conversation with Dad today. We've been tiptoeing around the subject of his retirement for months, but today I finally voiced my concerns about his health and the stress his job is causing him. It didn't go as badly as I feared, but it wasn't easy either.

I'm proud of myself for speaking up. A year ago, I would have kept quiet, and let the worry eat at me. This is growth, I suppose. Uncomfortable, but necessary. Dad seemed surprised at first, maybe a bit defensive, but as we talked, I could see him softening. He admitted he's been thinking about retirement too, but the idea scares him. We agreed to investigate some financial planning resources together.

This conversation is making me think about my own future. Am I setting myself up for a sustainable career? Or am I heading down the same path of overwork and stress? Something to ponder and perhaps act on.

It's strange to see Dad vulnerable. He's always been the strong one, the provider. But there's strength in vulnerability too, in being open to change. I hope I can support him through this transition the way he's always supported me.

Note to self: Call Dad next week. Maybe suggest a fishing trip like we used to do when I was a kid. It would be good for both of us to reconnect away from the pressures of daily life.

Tip: In reflective journaling, try to go beyond just recounting events. Explore your thoughts, feelings, and insights about the experience. Ask yourself questions like "Why did I react this way?" or "What can I learn from this?"

5. CREATIVE WRITING JOURNAL ENTRY

Date: June 21, 2027

Prompt: Write a six-word story about hope

Planted seeds. Watered daily. Flowers bloomed.

Expansion:

Sometimes hope is a slow, quiet process. It's the daily acts of faith, the persistent belief that our efforts matter, even when we can't see immediate results. Like tending a garden, nurturing hope requires patience, dedication, and trust in the unseen processes of growth.

In my own life, I've been "planting seeds" of change - small, consistent actions towards my goals. Some days it feels like nothing is happening. But then, I see progress. A small "bloom" of success, a tiny breakthrough. It reminds me to keep going, to keep nurturing my dreams and aspirations.

Hope isn't always about grand gestures or dramatic transformations. Often, it's about the quiet persistence of showing up day after day, believing in the potential for growth and beauty, even in the face of doubt or adversity.

Today, I choose to water my seeds of hope. What flowers might bloom if I remain patient and persistent?

Tip: Use creative writing prompts to spark new ideas and perspectives in your journaling. They can be a great way to explore your thoughts and feelings from a different angle.

Remember, these are just examples. Your journal entries will be unique to you, reflecting your own thoughts, experiences, and writing style. The most important thing is to write on a regular basis and to be honest, allowing your journal to be a true reflection of your inner world.

APPENDIX C: DIGITAL TOOLS AND APPLICATIONS FOR JOURNALING

1. DAYONE: THE ALL-IN-ONE JOURNAL

Sarah swiped open her phone, tapping the familiar book icon of the **DayOne** app. As she settled into her favorite coffee shop, the app automatically tagged her location and the current weather - sunny with a light breeze, perfect for an outdoor writing session.

She began typing:

"Another hectic day at the office, but taking this moment to breathe and reflect feels like a mini-vacation. The aroma of freshly brewed coffee and the gentle chatter around me are soothing my frazzled nerves..."

Sarah paused, then snapped a quick photo of her latte art to add to the entry. She loved how DayOne seamlessly integrated text, images, and metadata, creating a rich, multi-dimensional record of her life.

Later, scrolling through her past entries, Sarah marveled at how the app had captured her journey over the years. Each entry was a time capsule, complete with photos, locations, and even the music she was listening to at the time.

Tip: Experiment with DayOne's different templates and prompts. They can spark new ideas and help you maintain a consistent journaling habit.

2. NOTION: THE CUSTOMIZABLE JOURNALING POWERHOUSE

Alex stared at his **Notion** dashboard, a digital canvas of neatly organized blocks and databases. His journaling setup was a masterpiece of personalization:

- A daily log for quick thoughts and events
- A mood tracker with a colorful chart visualizing his emotional landscape over time
- A gratitude journal, each entry linked to relevant projects or areas of his life
- A dream journal, complete with tags for recurring themes and symbols

He clicked on today's daily log and began typing:

"Breakthrough on the Anderson project today! The team's collaborative brainstorming session yielded some innovative solutions. Note to self: explore the potential of AI integration further."

Alex then navigated to his "Big Ideas" database, quickly adding a new entry about AI in project management, and linking it to today's journal entry. He loved how Notion allowed him to connect ideas across different areas of his life and work.

Tip: Start with a simple Notion template and gradually customize it to fit your needs. The beauty of Notion is its flexibility - your journaling system can evolve as you do.

3. PENZU: THE SECURE DIGITAL DIARY

Emma bit her lip as she created a new entry in Penzu. This was going to be a difficult one to write, but she felt safe knowing that Penzu's military-grade encryption would keep her thoughts private.

She began pouring her heart out:

"I finally told Mom about my decision to change careers. It didn't go well. She thinks I'm throwing away years of hard work, but she doesn't understand how unfulfilled I've been..."

As Emma wrote, she felt the tension in her shoulders begin to ease. Penzu's clean, distraction-free interface helped her focus on her thoughts and emotions.

After finishing her entry, Emma used Penzu's tagging feature to categorize it under "Career" and "Family". She knew these tags would help her track this journey of career transition over time.

Tip: Use Penzu's reminder feature to maintain a consistent journaling habit. Set a daily reminder at a time when you're free and in a reflective mood.

4. JOURNEY: THE MULTIMEDIA MEMORY KEEPER

Mark opened the **Journey** app on his tablet, excited to document his ongoing adventure. As he sat in his tent, the sound of waves crashing on the beach in the background, he began a new entry:

"Day 15 of the coastal trek. The sunrise this morning was breathtaking - the sky exploded in shades of pink and orange, reflecting off the calm sea..."

Mark added a stunning photo of the sunrise, then recorded a short audio clip of the waves. He loved how Journey allowed him to capture his experiences in such a multi-sensory way.

Using the app's timeline feature, Mark scrolled back through his journey, each entry a vibrant memory brought to life through photos, videos, and audio clips. It was like reliving the adventure all over again.

Tip: Experiment with Journey's different media options. Sometimes a photo or audio clip can capture a moment better than words alone.

5. DIARO: THE ORGANIZED MEMORY BANK

Lisa opened Diaro on her laptop, ready to process the day's events. She appreciated how the app's folder structure helped her keep different aspects of her life organized.

She navigated to her "Work" folder and started a new entry:

"Project Phoenix update: We're falling behind schedule. Budget constraints are forcing us to cut corners, which doesn't sit well with me. Need to brainstorm alternative solutions..."

After writing, Lisa added tags like "Project Phoenix", "Challenges", and "Ethical Concerns". She knew these tags would help her track the project's progress and her own ethical journey in her career.

Using Diaro's powerful search function, Lisa then pulled up all entries related to work-life balance. She was preparing for a performance review and wanted to reflect on how she'd been managing her time over the past year.

Tip: Use Diaro's data visualization features to gain insights into your journaling habits and the themes that recur in your life.

Remember, the best digital journaling tool is the one that you'll use consistently. Each of these apps offers unique features, so don't be afraid to try several until you find the one that fits your journaling style and needs. Happy digital journaling!

APPENDIX D: JOURNALING FOR SPECIFIC PURPOSES

1. JOURNALING FOR MENTAL HEALTH

Sarah's hand trembled as she opened her journal. Today had been particularly difficult, with anxiety threatening to overwhelm her. She took a deep breath and began to write:

"June 15, 2025

Anxiety level: 8/10

Triggers: Upcoming presentation at work, argument with Mom

I can feel the familiar tightness in my chest, like a rubber band stretching to its limit. Thoughts are racing: Will I mess up the presentation? Does Mom think I'm a disappointment? Breathe, Sarah. Let's break this down:

1. *Presentation fears:*

   - *Fact: I've prepared thoroughly*
   - *Fact: My last presentation was well-received*

- *Action: Practice once more tomorrow, then trust in my preparation*

2. Argument with Mom:

- *Fact: We both said things in anger*
- *Fact: Mom has always supported me, even when we disagree*
- *Action: Call her tomorrow, apologize for my part, explain my feelings calmly*

Affirmation: I am capable and worthy. This anxiety is a feeling, not a fact. It will pass.

Gratitude: Despite the anxiety, I'm grateful for my supportive team at work and for having a mom who cares, even if we clash sometimes.

Next steps: 10 minutes of deep breathing, then a warm bath with lavender oil."

Sarah closed her journal, already feeling the anxiety begin to loosen its grip. The act of externalizing her thoughts and creating an action plan helped her regain a sense of control.

 Tip: When journaling for anxiety, try to include facts that counter your anxious thoughts, as well as concrete actions you can take. This can help ground you in reality and give you a sense of agency.

2. JOURNALING FOR CREATIVE WRITING

Mark stared at the blank page, willing inspiration to strike. He was halfway through writing his first novel, but the words had stopped flowing. Sighing, he picked up his pen and began a dialogue with his inner critic:

"July 3, 2025
Inner Critic (IC): You're stuck. Face it, you're not a real writer.

Mark (M): I've written 40,000 words. That makes me a writer.

IC: But this chapter isn't working. You should just give up.

M: Or I could try a different approach. What if I...

[Mark starts brainstorming, his pen flying across the page]

1. *Switch perspectives? Tell this chapter from the antagonist's POV?*
2. *Flash forward? Show the consequences of this decision in the future?*
3. *Bring in a new character who challenges the protagonist's choice?*

Option 2 is intriguing. It could add tension and give readers a glimpse of what's at stake. Let's try a quick sketch:

The courthouse loomed before Ella, its stone facade a silent witness to the countless lives changed within its walls. Five years had passed since that fateful night, but as she climbed the steps, the weight of her decision pressed down on her as heavily as ever...

Yes! I can work with this. It breaks me out of the linear narrative and adds a layer of foreboding to the current timeline.

Note to self: Don't let perfectionism paralyze you. Sometimes you need to write badly to write well. Keep pushing forward!"

Mark set down his pen, energized. What had started as a journaling exercise to overcome writer's block had turned into a breakthrough for his novel.

Tip: Use your journal as a sandbox for your creative writing. Feel free to experiment, play with different ideas, and silence your inner critic. Sometimes the best ideas come from uninhibited exploration.

3. JOURNALING FOR PROFESSIONAL DEVELOPMENT

Elena opened her career journal, determined to make sense of her recent job interview. She had prepared thoroughly, but something had felt off during the conversation. It was time to unpack the experience:

"August 18, 2025
Interview Analysis: Senior Marketing Manager at TechNova

What went well:

- *Articulated my experience with data-driven marketing strategies*
- *Connected my previous projects to TechNova's current challenges*
- *Asked insightful questions about company culture and growth opportunities*

Areas for improvement:

- *Stumbled when discussing my experience with AI-driven campaigns*
- *Could have provided more concrete examples of leadership experience*
- *Felt nervous during the salary negotiation discussion*

Unexpected questions:

1. *"How would you handle a team member who disagrees with your strategy?"*

My answer was okay but could have been stronger. Research conflict resolution strategies in leadership.

2. *"Where do you see the future of AR in marketing?*

Realized my knowledge of AR is outdated. Action item: Take an online course on emerging tech in marketing.

Insights:

- *Need to work on projecting more confidence, especially when discussing compensation.*
- *My technical skills are solid, but my leadership experience needs more emphasis.*
- *The company seems to value innovation highly - how can I position myself as a forward-thinker?*

Next steps:

1. *Send a thank-you email highlighting my enthusiasm for TechNova's innovative approach*
2. *Reach out to my mentor to roleplay salary negotiations*
3. *Start a side project incorporating AR to build hands-on experience*
4. *Review the job description again - are there any key requirements I can strengthen?*

Remember: Every interview is a learning experience. Regardless of the outcome, I've gained valuable insights to fuel my professional growth."

Elena closed her journal, feeling a renewed sense of purpose. While the interview may not have been perfect, she now had a clear plan to strengthen her candidacy, both for this position and future opportunities.

Tip: Use your professional development journal to track patterns in your career journey. Regular reflection can help you identify your strengths, areas for growth, and the types of roles or projects that excite you.

Remember, these are just a few examples of how journaling can be adapted for specific purposes. The beauty of journaling lies in its flexibility - you can tailor your practice to serve whatever goal or need you have in your life. Whether you're managing your mental health, fueling your creativity, or advancing your career, your journal can be a powerful tool for growth and self-discovery.

QUICK START GUIDE: YOUR FIRST WEEK OF JOURNALING

DAY 1: CHOOSING YOUR MEDIUM

Sarah stood in the stationery store, overwhelmed by the options. Leather-bound journals, spiral notebooks, and sleek digital tablets vied for her attention. After much deliberation, she chose a simple, hardcover notebook with cream-colored pages. The weight of it in her hands felt right, promising.

At home, she opened to the first page, uncapped her favorite pen, and wrote:

"August 1, 2025. My journaling journey begins today. I'm not sure where this will lead, but I'm excited to find out."

Tip: There's no "perfect" journaling medium. Choose what feels comfortable and inspiring to you, whether it's pen and paper or a digital app.

DAY 2: SETTING A ROUTINE

The alarm chimed at 6:30 AM. Alex groaned, tempted to hit snooze, but remembered his commitment to morning journaling. He dragged himself out of bed, made a cup of coffee, and settled into the cozy armchair by the window.

As the sun peeked over the horizon, he began to write:

"It's early, and I'm tired, but there's something peaceful about this moment. The house is quiet, the day is full of possibility..."

Twenty minutes flew by, and Alex was surprised to find himself energized and clear-headed, ready to face the day.

Tip: Experiment with different times of day for journaling. Some people prefer mornings for setting intentions, while others like evenings for reflection. Find what works best for your schedule and energy levels.

DAY 3: STARTING WITH A PROMPT

Emma stared at the blank page, unsure where to begin. She decided to try a prompt she'd read about:

"What would you do if you knew you couldn't fail?"

She began writing, hesitantly at first, then with increasing flow:

"If I couldn't fail, I'd quit my job and open that bakery I've always dreamed about. I'd create amazing, unique flavors and..."

An hour later, Emma looked up, surprised at how much she'd written and the insights she'd uncovered about her secret aspirations.

Tip: Keep a list of prompts handy for days when you're not sure what to write about. They can be great jumping-off points for exploration.

DAY 4: FREE WRITING

Mark set a timer for 10 minutes and began to write without stopping, letting his thoughts flow unfiltered onto the page:

"Feeling stressed about the project deadline wonder if I'll finish in time maybe I should ask for an extension but what if they think I can't handle it the weather's nice today I should go for a walk later clear my head..."

When the timer beeped, Mark reread his entry. Amid the stream of consciousness, he noticed recurring themes of work stress and a desire for nature. He made a note to prioritize outdoor time as a stress-management strategy.

Tip: Don't worry about grammar, punctuation, or even making sense during free writing. The goal is to bypass your inner critic and tap into your subconscious thoughts.

DAY 5: GRATITUDE JOURNALING

After a challenging day, Zoe opened her journal and decided to focus on gratitude. She wrote:

"Today, I'm grateful for:

1. *The colleague who brought me coffee when I was swamped with work*
2. *My comfortable bed that I get to come home to*
3. *The funny text from my sister that made me laugh*
4. *My health, which allows me to navigate daily challenges*
5. *The beautiful sunset I saw on my commute home"*

As she finished writing, Zoe noticed her mood had lifted. The day's frustrations didn't disappear, but they felt more manageable in the context of these positive aspects of her life.

Tip: Try to be specific in your gratitude entries. Instead of "I'm grateful for my friend," you might write "I'm grateful for the way my friend listened without judgment when I needed to vent."

DAY 6: REFLECTION AND PROBLEM-SOLVING

David used his journal to tackle a decision he'd been struggling with. He created two columns:

"Should I accept the job offer?

Pros: Cons:
- Higher salary - Longer commute
- More responsibility - Less creative freedom
- Prestigious company - High-stress environment
- Opportunity for advancement. - Less time with family"

As he wrote, David realized that his values of creativity and work-life balance were taking precedence over prestige and advancement. This clarity helped him lean towards declining the offer, a decision he felt at peace with.

Tip: Your journal can be a powerful tool for decision-making. Writing out your thoughts can help you see situations objectively and align choices with your values.

DAY 7: REVIEW AND REFLECT

On Sunday evening, Lisa reread her week's entries. She was surprised by the insights she'd gained and the patterns she noticed. She wrote a reflection:

"Looking back on this week of journaling, I'm amazed at how much I've discovered about myself. I've uncovered a passion project idea, identified a key source of stress, and reconnected with my gratitude practice. I'm excited to continue this journey and see where it leads."

She then set an intention for the coming week:

"This week, I want to explore my creativity more. I'll try adding sketches to my journal entries and perhaps do some free writing about that business idea that keeps popping up."

Tip: Establishing a routine to review your journal entries can help you notice patterns, track progress, and set intentions for future growth. Consider doing a weekly or monthly review.

Remember, this is just the beginning of your journaling journey. There's no "right" way to journal – the best practice is the one that works for you and that you can maintain consistently. Be patient with yourself, stay curious, and enjoy the process of self-discovery!

NOTE FROM THE AUTHOR

Dear Reader,

Thank you for investing your valuable time in this book. I trust that these insights and principles have provided you with practical tools for your personal, professional, or spiritual journey.

Your engagement with this material means a great deal, and I'd be grateful if you'd consider sharing your experience with others. Would you take a moment to leave an honest review? Your feedback not only helps others discover these resources but also contributes to our collective growth and learning.

Your insights can be shared on any of these platforms:

📚 Amazon ⭐ Goodreads 🍎 Apple Books 📖 Google Play Books

Want to stay connected? I'd love to keep you updated on new releases and exclusive content:

- Subscribe to weekly insights: Richard's Newsletter
- Access free resources: RichardFrench.Net

With appreciation for your commitment to growth,

Richard French

ABOUT THE AUTHOR

Richard French, a pioneering technology leader and entrepreneur, brings his wealth of experience in innovation and personal growth to the realm of journaling. As a driving force behind several successful technology companies, Richard has consistently demonstrated the power of self-reflection and clear goal-setting in achieving remarkable business transformations.

With a career spanning software, AI, and global business leadership, Richard has guided organizations from startup stage to multi-million dollar enterprises. His philosophy that "people work with us, not for us" underlies his approach to personal development and team building.

A mathematics graduate and GT race car driver, Richard combines analytical thinking with a passion for pushing boundaries. In "Write Your Way," he applies his unique perspective on goal achievement and self-expression, offering readers a roadmap to personal transformation drawn from his experiences in the fast-paced worlds of technology and motorsports.

Richard's insights, honed through years of leading innovation and speaking at industry conferences, now guide readers on their journey of self-discovery through the power of journaling.

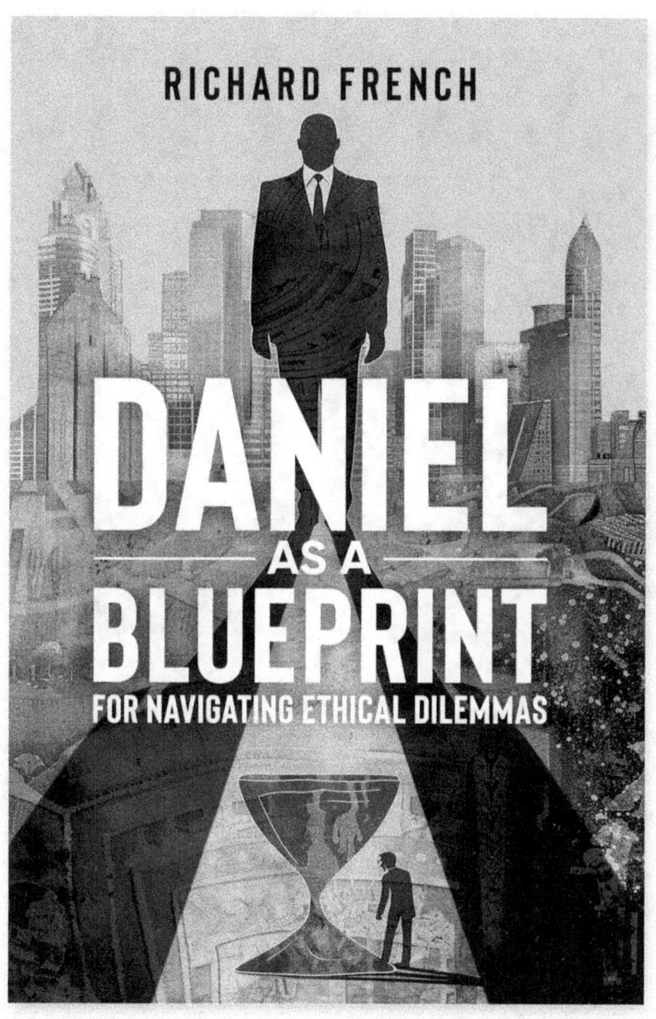

RICHARD FRENCH
DANIEL
AS A
BLUEPRINT
FOR NAVIGATING ETHICAL DILEMMAS

PROVERBS

— FOR —

PROFIT

ANCIENT WISDOM FOR MODERN BUSINESS ETHICS

RICHARD FRENCH

VERSE BY VERSE
REVELATION EXPLAINED
RICHARD FRENCH

THE
Art
OF
JOURNALING
A COMPREHENSIVE GUIDE TO
WRITING A JOURNAL
RICHARD FRENCH

Write
YOUR WAY
A COMPREHENSIVE GUIDE TO PERSONAL GROWTH
AND SELF-EXPRESSION THROUGH JOURNALING
2ND EDITION
CONTAINS NEW CHAPTER ON AI-ENHANCED JOURNALING
RICHARD FRENCH

THE YEAR-END REFLECTION GUIDE

A WRITE YOUR WAY JOURNALING BONUS

RICHARD FRENCH

ADVANCED PATTERN RECOGNITION

AN ART OF JOURNALING BONUS GUIDE

RICHARD FRENCH